EDUCAUSE

EDUCAUSE is an international, nonprofit association dedicated to transforming higher education through information technologies. The incorporation of EDUCAUSE in 1998 was the result of a consolidation of two prominent higher education technology associations—CAUSE and Educom—that recognized an increasing convergence in their missions and goals. The consolidated association has offices in Boulder, Colorado, and Washington, D.C.

EDUCAUSE

- provides professional development opportunities for those involved with planning for, managing, and using information technologies in colleges and universities
- seeks to influence policy by working with leaders in the education, corporate, and government sectors who have a stake in the transformation of higher education through information technologies
- enables the transfer of leading-edge approaches to information technology management and use that are developed and shared through EDUCAUSE policy and strategy initiatives
- provides a forum for dialog between information resources professionals and campus leaders at all levels
- informs members about IT innovations, strategies, and practices that may affect their campuses, identifying and researching the most pressing issues

For up-to-date information about EDUCAUSE programs, initiatives, and services visit the EDUCAUSE World Wide Web site at http://www.educause.edu.

PRICEWATERHOUSECOOPERS

PricewaterhouseCoopers is a leading provider of professional services to institutions of higher education. PwC serves a full range of educational institutions—from small colleges to large public and private universities to educational companies.

PricewaterhouseCoopers (www.pwcglobal.com), the world's largest professional services organization, helps its clients build value, manage risk, and improve their performance.

Drawing on the talents of more than 140,000 people in 152 countries, PricewaterhouseCoopers provides a full range of business advisory services to leading global, national, and local companies and to public institutions. These services include audit, accounting, and tax advice; management, information technology, and human resource consulting; financial advisory services; and business process outsourcing services.

Dancing with the Devil

Richard N. Katz and Associates

Dancing with the Devil

Information Technology and the New Competition in Higher Education

Jossey-Bass Publishers
San Francisco

Jossey-Bass books and products are available through most bookstores. To contact Jossey-Bass directly, call (888) 378-2537, fax to (800) 605-2665, or visit our website at www.josseybass.com.

Substantial discounts on bulk quantities of Jossey-Bass books are available to corporations, professional associations, and other organizations. For details and discount information, contact the special sales department at Jossey-Bass.

 Manufactured in the United States of America on Lyons Falls Turin Book. This paper is acid-free and 100 percent totally chlorine-free.

Library of Congress Cataloging-in-Publication Data

Dancing with the devil : information technology and the new competition in higher education / Richard N. Katz and associates — 1st ed.
    p. cm. — (The Jossey-Bass higher and adult education series)
Includes bibliographical references and index.
ISBN 0-7879-4695-8 (paperback)
1. Universities and colleges—United States—Administration. 2. Information technology—United States. 3. Education, Higher—Effect of technological innovations on—United States. 4. Competition—United States. 5. Educational change—United States. I. Katz, Richard N. II. Series.
LB2341 .D287 1999
378.73—ddc21   98–40098

PB Printing 10 9 8 7 6 5 4 3   FIRST EDITION

Contents

Acknowledgments

I would like to thank the contributors to this book, each of whom spent countless hours researching, preparing, and writing their chapters. They are dedicated professionals who gave willingly of their time and experience in the hopes that their work and thought might assist others in higher education.

We all owe a debt of thanks to EDUCAUSE for underwriting the effort that went into this volume. (EDUCAUSE was incorporated in July 1998 as a result of the consolidation of two major higher education technology associations, CAUSE and Educom.) In the early stages of the development of this volume, Jane N. Ryland, recently retired CAUSE president, and the members of the CAUSE board of directors were a constant source of support. EDUCAUSE founding president Brian L. Hawkins has continued this support and is committed to providing continued thought leadership to higher education policymakers and practitioners. Julia A. Rudy, EDUCAUSE director of research and development, played an indispensable role in bringing this volume to fruition. She is simply the best editor imaginable and shares the authors' love of higher education.

The firm of PricewaterhouseCoopers, LLP, has been a good friend of EDUCAUSE and an important partner in higher education. Jillinda J. Kidwell, the firm's higher education consulting practice leader, has been my steadfast friend and has underwritten a number of ventures designed to instigate and improve higher education's dialogue on emerging issues. The generous support of PricewaterhouseCoopers makes it possible for EDUCAUSE to share this volume with the information technology leaders of more than 1,500 colleges and universities.

I have written much and have never taken the opportunity to thank Peggy Rogers and Tony Clyde. Perhaps I have failed in this because of the awkwardness of juggling three last names within the same family. Peggy and Tony support, without condoning, my unusual hours and penchant to surround myself (and them) with manuscripts and other works in progress. I owe them a lot.

R. N. K.

Preface

Many of the readers of this volume may think of higher education's relationship with information technology as a dance with the devil. For many years, campus information technologists have struggled to place the object of their affection on their chancellors' and presidents' agenda. That time has come. Many of us in higher education now wish that we could push the information technology genie back into the bottle, as this technology is raising cultural, organizational, economic, and even survival issues for which the questions greatly outweigh the answers.

College and university leaders need answers. Investments of unprecedented magnitude and risk need to be made. The information available to inform these decisions is too often superfluous, self-aggrandizing, obtuse, or contradictory. As information technologies and resources pervade our institutions, the interrelationships among campus citizens, capital resources, technologies, and practices form a crazy quilt that befuddles analysis and decision making. Simple but necessary leadership questions such as "what will this cost?" or "who will receive what benefits?" become difficult to answer. This morass can foster either inaction or reluctant action on recommendations that are poorly understood.

Dancing with the devil once should be enough for anyone in our industry. Not only have we failed to master the complex steps and rhythms of distance education, distributed learning, virtual campuses, digital libraries, and the like, but we must now attempt to achieve this mastery in the context of burgeoning competition. The emergence of the Information Age is presenting educators, leaders, and policymakers with unprecedented challenges and opportunities. The *promise* of the Information Age is the delivery of information "anytime, anywhere." The *premise* of the Information Age is the highly educated "knowledge worker." Can we speculate that our existing higher education infrastructure is the *precondition* of the Information Age? Perhaps not. Davis and Botkin, in their book *The Monster Under the Bed* (Simon & Schuster, 1994), argued that private firms, frustrated with colleges' and universities' inability to meet the continuing educational needs of the knowledge workforce, will be forced to assume a large (and profitable) portion of higher education's instructional mission. Perhaps it is a coincidence that private firms like Sun (SunU), Arthur D. Little (Arthur D. Little School of Management), Dell (Dell University), International Thomson (Thomson University), Ericsson (Ericsson Wireless University), and others have begun to appropriate the linguistic icons of higher education. Some pundits and industry analysts refer to the emergence of a "higher learning" industry, dominated by commercial firms.

This volume was conceived and developed to frame the questions presented by emerging technologies and competition in ways that will make it possible for higher education's leaders to organize plans and actions to move their institutions forward. The chapters in this volume were written by a group of internationally regarded leaders in higher education. In particular, we have assembled a team of practitioners whose perspectives draw from experience as university executives, faculty, information technologists, academic administrators, and commercial providers.

Common threads can be traced throughout the fabric of this volume. The first and dominant thread, of course, is change—change to higher education enabled by, or even driven by, information technology. In Chapter One, University of Michigan president emeritus James J. Duderstadt speculates that "higher education is likely to evolve from a loosely federated system of colleges and universities serving traditional students from local communities into, in effect, a knowledge and learning industry." Industry executives Harvey Blustain, Philip Goldstein, and Gregory Lozier state boldly in Chapter Three that "the ivory tower is under siege." In Chapter Four, Lehigh University president Gregory C. Farrington claims that "digital media are now challenging those most venerable institutions—colleges and universities—to rethink the ways in which they serve society."

A second thread is the authors' shared belief that colleges' and universities' unique economic standing as quasi monopolies is at risk. Although few agree that the potential of networked information to diminish the importance of time and place will render our campuses obsolete, this volume, if successful, challenges the reader to view new investment in traditional cost drivers (for example, physical plants) as strategic choices and not as imperatives. New competitors in select areas of undergraduate, adult, and specialized education and training are responding to perceived financial opportunity in domains that were previously reserved for traditional educators. Despite the likely growth in overall demand for postsecondary education globally, newly accredited purveyors—rich in cash and technology and unencumbered by tradition, bricks, and mortar—will seek to deliver those high-yield courses that currently subsidize much of today's educational enterprise.

The third thread in this volume is that of hope. The authors share an unwavering belief in higher education's mission and in the capacity of colleges and universities to renew themselves continually in the face of new opportunities and challenges. Although new technologies and competition will likely threaten those institutions that do not make wise strategic choices, these forces will permit many others to extend their mission, to enhance the quality of their offerings, and to enrich the experience of learning and scholarship.

This volume has been organized not only to frame problems but also to suggest solutions. James Duderstadt raises the question of survival directly and establishes the context for change by describing the variety and intensity of challenges facing higher education leaders and their institutions.

My chapter (Chapter Two) focuses specifically on information technology as one of the drivers of needed change and concludes that the combination of pressures posed by competition and information technology suggest the need for concerted institutional strategy setting in this new context. New competition and information will impel institutions to rethink their instructional products and, in particular, their markets, forcing a host of sensitive campus and public policy issues to the fore.

Harvey Blustain, Philip Goldstein, and Gregory Lozier assess higher education's competitive landscape and provide a specific framework for institutions to engage in institutional strategy making. These authors present their readers with a management model and a set of questions that campus leaders can use to guide their institutions through a process of self-illumination that can inform investment decisions and actions.

Gregory Farrington provides an assessment of the specific impact of new information technologies on the future of residential undergraduate education. He concludes that although institutions must change, "the most imaginative colleges and universities will not hesitate to use the new technologies to make education more effective, more affordable, and more accessible."

William Graves's chapter (Chapter Five) presents campus leaders with an investment framework and organizational model to guide the increasingly complex and problematic investment in campus information technology and resources. He describes a set of compelling principles and an information technology life cycle model that guide not only investment decisions but also campus organizational responses and partnership strategies.

For better or worse, we live in interesting times. The Information Age is being fueled by knowledge and driven by the so-called knowledge worker. A higher education, in this context, is no longer a luxury. Our venerable institutions have the potential to assume positions of increased centrality within the communities we serve. This heightened centrality, and the associated revenue opportunities, is attracting new competition. The challenge facing higher education's leaders is daunting, and the stakes are high.

The contributors to this volume hope that we have in small measure framed the issues of information technology and competition in ways that will enrich the dialogue on college and university campuses. We hope, especially, that some of the recommended principles, frameworks, and approaches offered here will inspire those actions that will ensure existing colleges and universities a continued central role in an exciting future.

Boulder, Colorado   Richard N. Katz
September 1998

The Authors

Richard N. Katz is vice president of EDUCAUSE. He is responsible for developing and delivering the association's educational program through a variety of international conferences, workshops, seminars, institutes, and publications, as well as for member and corporate relations, research and development, and outreach. Prior to joining the association in 1996, Katz held a variety of management and executive positions, spanning fourteen years, at the University of California (UC). As executive director of business planning and practices, he was responsible for the design and implementation of many of the nine-campus UC system's strategic management initiatives. At UC, Katz was awarded the Gurevich Prize and the Olsten Award and was the second recipient of the university's Award for Innovative Management and Leadership. He has been the author, coauthor, or editor of more than twenty books, monographs, and articles on a variety of management and technology topics. Katz received his B.S. degree from the University of Pittsburgh and his M.B.A from UCLA.

Harvey Blustain is director of the Higher Education Consulting Practice at PricewaterhouseCoopers. He has over fifteen years' consulting experience in a range of industries, including higher education, telecommunications, high technology, health care and insurance, commercial and industrial manufacturing, financial services, agriculture, and government. Blustain has helped clients in a number of areas, such as leadership development, executive coaching, process reengineering, organizational development, competency-based human resource development, and training. He has authored over three dozen professional publications, including *Performance Appraisal: Legal and Effective Management of Performance* and *Outplacement in Times of Organizational Change*. Blustain has a Ph.D. and M.Phil. from Yale University and a B.A. from New York University.

James J. Duderstadt is president emeritus and university professor of science and engineering at the University of Michigan. Duderstadt also serves as director of the Millennium Project, a research center concerned with the future of higher education. He received his baccalaureate degree from Yale University in 1964 and his doctorate in engineering science and physics from the California Institute of Technology in 1967. After serving for twelve years on the faculty of the University of Michigan, he was named dean of engineering and later provost and vice president for academic affairs. He was elected president of the university in 1988 and served in that role until July 1996. Duderstadt has received numerous national awards, including the E.O. Lawrence Award for excellence in nuclear research, the Arthur Holly Compton Prize for outstanding teaching, and the National Medal of Technology for exemplary service. He has been elected to numerous honorific societies, including the National Academy of Engineering, and has served on and/or chaired numerous boards, including the National Science Board.

Gregory C. Farrington is president of Lehigh University and professor of materials science and engineering. From 1990 to 1998 he was dean of the School of Engineering and Applied Science at the University of Pennsylvania. Farrington's principal research interests are in the areas of electrochemistry, solid electrolytes, and solid state chemistry. He is the author or coauthor of more than one hundred papers on the synthesis, structure, and transport characteristics of conductive ceramics and polymers and holds twenty-seven patents. Farrington has served as a member of the Carnegie Foundation Commission on National Security and the Future of Arms Control, the Materials Research Advisory Committee of the National Science Foundation, and the Council of the Materials Research Society and was president of the International Society of Solid State Ionics. Farrington has been very active on issues relating to the new uses of computer and information technology in education. He received a bachelor's degree from Clarkson University in 1968 and a Ph.D. in chemistry from Harvard University in 1972. In 1984 Farrington was awarded an honorary Ph.D. by the University of Uppsala, Sweden, in recognition of his research in solid state electrochemistry.

Philip Goldstein is a principal in the Higher Education Consulting Practice at PricewaterhouseCoopers. He has more than seven years' experience as a consultant to the higher education industry, with a focus on business process reengineering, organizational design, and technology implementation. Goldstein has been a frequent speaker on outsourcing in higher education at the annual meetings of the National Association of College and University Business Officers (NACUBO), the Association of Higher Education Facilities Officers (APPA), and the National Association of College Auxiliary Services (NACAS). He has also coauthored a monograph, *Contract Management or Self-Operation: A Decision-Making Guide for Higher Education*, with Daphne Kempner for the Council of Higher Education Management Associations. Goldstein received a B.A. degree in economics from Brandeis University and an M.B.A from the New York University Stern School of Business.

William H. Graves is president of the nonprofit COLLEGIS Research Institute and senior vice president and member of the board of directors of COLLEGIS, a higher education information technology service company. Graves came to his present position after thirty years at the University of North Carolina at Chapel Hill, where he was a professor, chief information officer, and founder and director of the Institute for Academic Technology. He has been a member of the Board of Directors of CAUSE and is currently a member of the EDUCAUSE Board. Graves chairs the planning committee for EDUCAUSE's National Learning Infrastructure Initiative and also serves on the steering committees for the Instructional Management Systems(IMS) Cooperative and the Coalition for Networked Information. He served on the steering committee for the Internet2 Project and helped organize the University Corporation for Advanced Internet Development (UCAID). Graves has served as a consultant for many institutions as they plan a role for information technology services in shaping their future. He has delivered over 350 invited presentations on campuses and at conferences and has published over forty articles. He earned his Ph.D. in mathematics at Indiana University.

Gregory Lozier is a managing associate in the Higher Education Consulting Practice at PricewaterhouseCoopers, with a focus on strategy formulation and implementation, budgeting, and academic restructuring. He has more than twenty-five years' experience in higher education administration, serving most recently as executive director of planning and analysis at The Pennsylvania State University. Lozier has consulted in more than twenty-five colleges, universities, and nonprofit organizations and in Europe, Africa, Hong Kong, Indonesia, and New Zealand. With over thirty publications, he also has been a frequent speaker and workshop presenter at national and regional conferences. Lozier received a bachelor's degree from Rutgers, a master's degree in education from Southern Illinois University, and a doctoral degree in education from The Pennsylvania State University.

Dancing with the Devil

Can Colleges and Universities Survive in the Information Age?

James J. Duderstadt

The next decade will represent a period of significant transformation for colleges and universities as we respond to the challenges of serving a changing society and a profoundly changed world. Perhaps the most critical challenges facing most institutions will be to develop the capacity for change; to remove the constraints that prevent institutions from responding to the needs of rapidly changing societies; to remove unnecessary processes and administrative structures; to question existing premises and arrangements; and to challenge, excite, and embolden all members of the campus community to embark on what I believe will be a great adventure.

Those institutions that can step up to this process of change will thrive. Those that bury their heads in the sand, that rigidly defend the status quo or—even worse—some idyllic vision of a past that never existed, are at very great risk. Those institutions that are micromanaged, either from within, by faculty politics or governing boards, or from without, by government or public opinion, stand little chance of flourishing during a time of great change.

There is no question that the need for learning institutions such as colleges and universities will become increasingly important in a knowledge-driven future. The real question is not whether higher education will be transformed but rather *how* and *by whom*. It is my belief that the challenge of change before us should be viewed not as a threat but as an opportunity for a renewal, perhaps even a renaissance in higher education. The decade before us could be—*should be*—one of the great adventures of our times.

Last year I had the privilege of cochairing a national conference concerned with the nature of the stresses on research and education in American higher education. Over the past couple of years, town hall meetings of faculty had been sponsored by the National Science Board and the National Academy of Sciences on dozens of campuses. The goal of the national conference was to pull all of this together in discussion with representatives of the federal government. The key issues raised by the faculty and administrators were, for the most part, the obvious ones:

- Fears about the future funding of research

- The stresses of grantsmanship

- The loss, with increasing specialization, of a sense of scholarly community

- The imbalance between the rewards given research versus those accorded teaching

- A host of management issues, such as indirect costs, facilities support, government reporting and accountability requirements, and so on

Interestingly enough, the impact of information technology on the academy did not even appear on the radar scope. Yet from these meetings it was also clear that the concerns expressed were simply symptoms of the impact of more fundamental forces driving change, many of which relate directly to emerging digital technology.

The Forces of Change

There are many ways to group the challenges of change in higher education. Let me suggest the following framework.

Financial Imperatives

Since the late 1970s, higher education in America has been caught in a financial vise (Dionne and Kean, 1997). On the one hand, the magnitude of the services demanded of colleges and universities has grown considerably; on the other hand, the costs of providing such services have grown at an even faster rate. These activities are dependent on a highly skilled, professional workforce (faculty and staff), require expensive new facilities and equipment, and are driven by an ever-expanding knowledge base.

As the demand for educational services grew over the past two decades and operating costs rose, public support for higher education flattened and then declined (Breneman, Finney, and Roherty, 1997). The growth in state support of public higher education peaked in the 1980s and now has fallen in many states. And although the federal government has sustained its support of research, growth has been modest in recent years and is likely to decline as discretionary domestic spending comes under increasing pressure from federal-budget-balancing efforts. The new federal budget agreement may be good news to middle-class parents, but it is unlikely to bring new resources to higher education.

To meet growing societal demand for higher education at a time when costs are increasing and public support is declining, most institutions have been forced to sharply increase tuition and fees, triggering public concern about the costs and availability of a college education. As a result, most colleges and universities are now looking for ways to control costs and increase productivity, but most are also finding that their current organization and governance makes this very difficult. It seems increasingly clear that the higher education enterprise in America must change dramatically if it is to restore a balance between the costs and availability of educational services needed by our society and the resources available to support these services.

Societal Needs

Yet the needs of our society for the services provided by our colleges and universities will continue to grow. Significant expansion will be necessary just to respond to the needs of a growing population that will produce a 30 percent increase in the number of college-age students over the next two decades. Beyond this traditional role, we should recognize the impact of the changing nature of the educational services sought by our society.

Today's undergraduate student body is no longer dominated by eighteen- to twenty-two-year-old high school graduates from affluent backgrounds. Increasing numbers of adults from diverse socioeconomic backgrounds, already in the workplace and perhaps with families, are seeking the education and skills necessary for their careers. To meet the demands of this growing population, existing institutions will have to change significantly, or new types of institutions will have to be formed.

We are beginning to see a shift in demand from the current style of "just-in-case" education, in which we expect students to complete degree programs at the undergraduate or professional level long before they actually need the knowledge, to "just-in-time" education, in which education is sought when a person needs it through nondegree programs, to "just-for-you" education, in which educational programs are carefully tailored to meet the specific lifelong learning requirements of particular students. Likewise, we are seeing a shift from synchronous, classroom-based instruction to asynchronous, computer network–based learning to the provision of ubiquitous learning opportunities throughout our society. Both shifts will demand major change.

The nature of the needs for other higher education services also is changing dramatically. The relationship between the federal government and the research university is shifting from a partnership, in which the government is primarily a patron of discovery-oriented research, to a process of procurement of research aimed at addressing specific national priorities. The academic medical center has come under great financial pressure as it has been forced to deal with a highly competitive health care marketplace and the entry of new paradigms such as managed care. Although the public appetite for the entertainment provided by intercollegiate athletics continues to grow, our colleges also feel increasing pressures to better align these activities with academic priorities and national imperatives (such as the Title IX requirements for gender equity).

Even as the nature of traditional activities in education, research, and service change, society is seeking new services from higher education: for example, revitalizing K–12 education, securing economic competitiveness, providing models for multicultural societies, and rebuilding our cities and national infrastructure. All of this is occurring at a time when public criticism of higher education is high and trust and confidence in the university is relatively low.

Technology Drivers

As knowledge-driven organizations, it is not surprising that colleges and universities should be greatly affected by the rapid advances in information technology—in computers, telecommunications, and networks. This technology has already had a dramatic impact on campus research activities, including the creation of an entirely new form of research: computer simulation of complex phenomena. Many administrative processes have become heavily dependent on information technology—as the current concern with the approaching "year 2000 problem" has made all too apparent. There is an increasing sense that information technology will have an even more profound impact in the future on the educational activities of colleges and universities and on how we deliver our services. To be sure, there have been earlier technology changes, such as television, but never before has there been such a rapid and sustained period of change with such broad social applications.

Most significant here is the way in which emerging information technology has removed the constraints of space and time. We can now use powerful computers and networks to deliver educational services to anyone at any place and any time, no longer confining education to the campus or the academic schedule. The market for college and university services is expanding rapidly, but so is competition, as new organizations such as virtual universities and "learning-ware" providers enter this marketplace to compete with traditional institutions.

Let me illustrate the role of emerging information technology as a driver of change in higher education by considering its impact in two areas: the changing nature of our fundamental academic activities and the changing nature of the higher education enterprise.

The Changing Nature of Academic Activities

It is common to refer to the primary missions of the university in terms of the honored trinity of teaching, research, and service. But these roles can also be regarded as simply the twentieth-century manifestations of the more fundamental roles of *creating, preserving, integrating, transmitting,* and *applying* knowledge. If we were to adopt the more contemporary language of computer networks, the college or university might be regarded as a "knowledge server," providing knowledge services (that is, creating, preserving, transmitting, or applying knowledge) in whatever form is needed by contemporary society.

From this more abstract viewpoint, it is clear that although these fundamental roles of the college or university do not change over time, the particular realization of these roles does change—and change quite dramatically, in fact.

Teaching

Consider, for example, the role of teaching. We generally think of this role in terms of a professor teaching a class of students, who in turn respond by reading assigned texts, writing papers, solving problems or performing experiments, and taking examinations. We should also recognize that classroom instruction is a relatively recent form of pedagogy. Throughout the last millennium, the more common form of learning was through apprenticeship. Both the neophyte scholar and craftsman learned by working as an apprentice to a master. Although this type of one-on-one learning still occurs today in skilled professions (such as medicine) and in advanced education (such as Ph.D. programs), it is simply too labor-intensive for the mass educational needs of modern society.

The classroom itself may soon be replaced by more appropriate and efficient learning experiences. Indeed, such a paradigm shift may be forced on faculty by the students themselves. Today's students are members of the "digital generation." They have spent their early lives surrounded by robust, visual, electronic media—*Sesame Street*, MTV, home computers, video games, cyberspace networks, MUDs, MOOs, and virtual reality. Unlike those of us who were raised in an era of passive, broadcast media such as radio and television, today's students expect—indeed, demand—interaction. They approach learning as a "plug-and-play" experience: they are unaccustomed and unwilling to learn sequentially—to read the manual—and instead are inclined to plunge in and learn through participation and experimentation. Although this type of learning is far different from the sequential, pyramidal approach of the traditional college or university curriculum, it may be far more effective for this generation, particularly when provided through a media-rich environment.

It could well be that faculty members of the twenty-first century college or university will find it necessary to set aside their roles as teachers and instead become designers of learning experiences, processes, and environments. Tomorrow's faculty may have to discard the present style of solitary learning experiences, in which students tend to learn primarily on their own through reading, writing, and problem solving. Instead, they may be asked to develop collective learning experiences, in which students work together and learn together, with the faculty member becoming more of a consultant or a coach than a teacher. Faculty members will be less concerned with identifying and then transmitting intellectual content and more focused on inspiring, motivating, and managing an active learning process by students. Here we should note that this will require a major change in graduate education, since few of today's faculty members have learned these skills.

Research

One can easily identify similarly profound changes occurring in the other roles of the research university. The process of creating new knowledge—of research and scholarship—is also evolving rapidly away from the solitary scholar to teams of scholars, perhaps spread over a number of disciplines. Is the concept of the disciplinary specialist really necessary—or even relevant—in a future in which the most interesting and significant problems will require "big think" rather than "small think"? Who needs such specialists when intelligent software agents will soon be available to roam far and wide through robust networks containing the knowledge of the world, instantly and effortlessly extracting whatever a person wishes to know?

There is also increasing pressure to draw research topics more directly from worldly experience than predominantly from the curiosity of scholars. Even the nature of knowledge creation is shifting somewhat away from the *analysis of what has been* to the *creation of what has never been*—drawing more on the experience of the artist than on the analytical skills of the scientist.

The Library

The preservation of knowledge is one of the most rapidly changing functions of colleges and universities. The computer—or, more precisely, the "digital convergence" of various media, from print to graphics to sound to sensory experiences to virtual reality—has already moved beyond the printing press in its impact on knowledge. Throughout the centuries, the intellectual focal point of the university has been its library, with its collection of written works preserving the knowledge of civilization. Today such knowledge exists in many forms—as text, graphics, sound, algorithms, and virtual reality simulations—and it exists almost literally in the ether, distributed in digital representations over worldwide networks, accessible by anyone, and certainly not the prerogative of the privileged few in academe.

Service

Finally, it is also clear that societal needs will continue to dictate great changes in the applications of knowledge expected from the university. Over the past several decades, society has asked higher education to serve in a broadening array of service roles, from providing health care to improving K–12 education, stimulating local economic development, and enriching our cultural resources.

The abstract definition of the "knowledge server" role of colleges and universities has existed throughout their long history and will certainly continue to exist as long as these remarkable social institutions survive. But the particular realization of the fundamental roles of knowledge creation, preservation, integration, transmission, and application will continue to change in profound ways, as they have so often done in the past. And the challenge of changing—of transforming—is in part a necessity simply to sustain our traditional roles in society.

The Changing Nature of the Higher Education Enterprise

Colleges and universities have long enjoyed a monopoly over advanced education because of geographical location and their monopoly on certification through the awarding of degrees. Today all of these market constraints are being challenged, as information technology eliminates the barriers of space and time and as new competitive forces enter the marketplace to challenge "credentialing."

In the current paradigm, our colleges and universities are faculty-centered. The faculty has long been accustomed to dictating what it wishes to teach, how it will teach it, and where and when the learning will occur. Students must travel to the campus to learn. They must work their way through the bureaucracy of university admissions, counseling, scheduling, and residential living. And they must pay for the privilege. If they complete the gauntlet of requirements, they are finally awarded a certificate to recognize their learning—a college degree. This process is sustained by accrediting associations, professional societies, and state and federal governments.

This carefully regulated and controlled enterprise could be eroded by several factors. First, the growing demand for advanced education and training simply cannot be met by such a carefully rationed and controlled paradigm. Second, current cost structures for higher education are simply incapable of responding to the need for high-quality yet affordable education. Third, information technology is releasing higher education from the constraints of space and time (and possibly also reality with virtual universities). All of these forces are driving us toward an open learning environment, in which the student will evolve into an active learner and consumer, and unleashing strong market forces.

Tomorrow's student will have access to a vast array of learning opportunities, far beyond what is offered by the faculty-centered institutions that characterize higher education today. Some will provide formal credentials; others will provide simply knowledge; still others will be available whenever the student—more precisely, the learner—needs the knowledge. The evolution toward such a learner-centered educational environment is both evident and irresistible.

As a result, higher education is likely to evolve from a loosely federated system of colleges and universities serving traditional students from local communities into, in effect, a knowledge and learning industry. Since nations throughout the world are experiencing growing needs and demands for advanced education, this industry will be global in extent. With the emergence of new competitive forces and the weakening influence of traditional constraints, higher education is evolving like other "deregulated" industries (for example, health care, communications, and energy). In contrast to these other industries, which have been restructured as government regulation of them has weakened, the global knowledge-learning industry will be unleashed by emerging information technology that frees education from the constraints of space, time, and credentialing monopolies.

Although many in the academy would undoubtedly view with derision or alarm the depiction of the higher education enterprise as an "industry" or "business," operating in a highly competitive, increasingly deregulated, global marketplace, this is nevertheless an important perspective that will require a new paradigm for postsecondary education. As our society becomes ever more dependent on new knowledge and educated people—on knowledge workers—this global knowledge business must be viewed clearly as one of the most active growth industries of our times. It is clear that no one, no government, will be in control of the higher education industry. It will respond to the forces of the marketplace.

Will this restructuring of the higher education enterprise really happen? If you doubt it, just consider the health care industry. While Washington debated federal programs to control health care costs and procrastinated about taking action, the marketplace took over with new paradigms such as managed care and for-profit health centers. In less than a decade, the health care industry was totally changed. Today, higher education is a $180–billion-a-year enterprise. It will almost certainly be "corporatized," similar to health care. By whom? By state or federal government? Not likely. By traditional institutions such as colleges and universities working through statewide systems or national alliances? Also unlikely. Or by the marketplace itself, as it did for health care, spawning new players such as virtual universities and for-profit educational organizations? Perhaps.

Last year a leading information services company visited with my institution to share with us their perspective on the higher education market. They believe the size of the higher education enterprise in the United States during the next decade could be as large as $300 billion per year, with thirty million students, roughly half composed of traditional students and the rest consisting of adult learners who are also in the workforce. (Incidentally, they also put the size of the world market at $3 trillion.) Their operational model of the brave new world of market-driven higher education suggests that this emerging domestic market for educational services could be served by a radically restructured enterprise consisting of fifty thousand faculty "content providers," two hundred thousand faculty "learning facilitators," and one thousand faculty "celebrities," who would be the stars of commodity learning-ware products. The learner would be linked to these faculty resources by an array of for-profit service companies handling the production and packaging of learning-ware, the distribution and delivery of these services to learners, and the assessment and certification of learning outcomes. Quite a contrast with the current enterprise!

Unbundling

The modern university has evolved into a monolithic institution that controls all aspects of learning. Universities provide courses at the undergraduate, graduate, and professional level; they support residential colleges, professional schools, lifelong learning, athletics, libraries, museums, and entertainment. They have assumed responsibility for all manner of activities beyond simply educating—housing and feeding students, providing police and other security protection, offering counseling and financial services, even operating power plants on many midwestern campuses!

Today, comprehensive universities are at considerable risk, at least as full-service organizations. These institutions have become highly vertically integrated. We are already beginning to see the growth of differentiated competitors for many of these activities. Universities are under increasing pressure to spin off, sell off, or close down parts of their traditional operations in the face of this new competition.

The most significant effect of the development of a deregulated higher education "industry" will be the breaking apart of this monolith, much as other industries have been broken apart through deregulation. As universities are forced to evolve from faculty-centered to learner-centered organizations, they may well find it necessary to unbundle their many functions, ranging from admissions and counseling to instruction and certification.

An example might be useful here. Consider the rapid growth of cyberspace, or virtual, universities, institutions without a campus or faculty that provide computer-mediated distance education. The virtual university might be viewed as the "Nike approach" to higher education. Nike, a major supplier of athletic shoes in the United States and worldwide, does not manufacture the shoes it markets. It has decided that its strength is in marketing and that it should outsource its manufacturing to those who can do it better and cheaper. In a sense, the virtual university similarly unbundles marketing and delivery. It works with the marketplace to understand needs, and then it outsources courses, curricula, and other educational services from established colleges and universities—or perhaps individual faculty—and delivers them through the use of sophisticated information technology.

There are many other examples. Although we are very good at producing intellectual content for education, there may be others who are far better at packaging and delivering that content. Although in the past colleges and universities have had a monopoly on certifying learning, there may be others, whether they be accreditation agencies or other kinds of providers, more capable of assessing and certifying that learning has occurred. Many of our other activities—for example, financial management and facilities management—are activities that might be outsourced to specialists.

Clearly higher education is an industry ripe for the unbundling of activities. Colleges and universities, like other institutions in our society, will have to come to terms with what their true strengths are, determine how those strengths support their strategies, and then be willing to outsource needed capabilities in areas where they do not have a unique competitive advantage.

The Emergence of a Commodity Market

Throughout most of its history, higher education has been a cottage industry. Individual courses are a handcrafted, made-to-order product. Faculty members design from scratch the courses they teach, whether they be for a dozen or several hundred students. They may use standard textbooks from time to time—although many do not—but their schedules, their lectures, their assignments, and their exams are developed for the particular course at the time it is taught. In a very real sense, the industrial age has largely passed the university by. Our social institutions for learning—schools, colleges, and universities—continue to favor programs and practices based more on past traditions than on contemporary needs.

Our ability to introduce new, more effective avenues for learning, not merely new media with which to convey information, will change the nature of higher education. The model of individually handcrafted course development may give way to a much more complex method of creating instructional materials. For example, entertainment companies with strong capabilities in packaging and distributing content might link with educational institutions with competence in content development. Even the standard packaging of an undergraduate education into "courses," required in the past by the need to have all the students in the same place at the same time, may no longer be necessary with new forms of asynchronous learning and interactive distance learning communities. Of course, it will be a challenge to break the handcrafted model while still protecting the traditional independence of the faculty to determine curricular content. There is also a long-standing culture in which faculty believe that they own the intellectual content of their courses and are free to market them to others for personal gain (for example, through textbooks or off-campus consulting services). But colleges and universities may have to restructure these paradigms and renegotiate ownership of the intellectual products represented by classroom courses if they are to constrain costs and respond to the needs of society.

As distributed virtual environments become more common, there may come a time when the classroom experience itself becomes a true commodity product, provided to anyone, anywhere, anytime—for a price. If students could actually obtain the classroom experience provided by some of the most renowned teachers in the world, why would they want to take classes from the local professor (or, in many cases, the local teaching assistant)? In such a commodity market, the role of the faculty member would change substantially. Rather than developing content and transmitting it in a classroom environment, a faculty member might instead have to manage a learning process in which students use an educational commodity—for example, the Microsoft Virtual "Life on Earth" Course, starring Stephen J. Gould. This would require a shift from the skills of intellectual analysis and classroom presentation to those of motivation, consultation, and inspiration. Welcome back, Mr. Chips!

Mergers, Acquisitions, and Hostile Takeovers

The perception of the higher education enterprise as a deregulated industry has several other implications. There are over 3,600 four-year colleges and universities in the United States, characterized by a great diversity in size, mission, constituencies, and funding sources. Not only are we likely to see the appearance of new educational entities in the years ahead, but as in other deregulated industries, there could well be a period of fundamental restructuring of the enterprise itself. Some colleges and universities might disappear. Others could merge. Some might actually acquire other institutions. One might even imagine a Darwinian process emerging, with some institutions devouring their competitors in "hostile takeovers." All such events have occurred in deregulated industries in the past, and all are possible in the future we envision for higher education.

The market forces unleashed by technology and driven by increasing demand for higher education are very powerful. If they are allowed to dominate and reshape the higher education enterprise, we could well find ourselves facing a world in which some of the most important values and traditions of the university have fallen by the wayside. Although the commercial, convenience-store model of the University of Phoenix may be a very effective way to meet the workplace skill needs of some adults, it certainly is not a paradigm that would be suitable for many of the higher purposes of the university. As we assess these market-driven emerging learning structures, we must bear in mind the importance of preserving the ability of the university to serve a broader public purpose.

The waves of market pressures on our colleges and universities are building, driven by the realities of our times: the growing correlation between one's education and quality of life, the strategic role of knowledge in determining the prosperity and security of nations, the inability of traditional higher education institutions to monopolize an open-learning marketplace characterized by active student-learner-consumers and rapidly evolving technology. Driven by an entrepreneurial culture, both within our institutions and across American society, the early phases of a restructuring of the higher education enterprise are beginning to occur.

Without a broader recognition of the growing learning needs of our society, an exploration of more radical learning paradigms, and an overarching national strategy that acknowledges the public purpose of higher education and the important values of the academy, higher education may be driven down roads that could lead to an erosion in quality. Many of the pressures on our public universities are similar to those that have contributed so heavily to the current plight of K–12 education in America. Furthermore, our experience with market-driven, media-based enterprises has not been reassuring. The broadcasting and publishing industries suggest that commercial concerns can lead to mediocrity, an intellectual wasteland in which the least common denominator of quality dominates.

Evolution or Revolution?

In spite of the growing awareness of these social forces, many within the academy still believe that change will occur only at the margins of higher education. They stress the role of colleges and universities in stabilizing society during a period of change rather than leading those changes. This, too, shall pass, they proclaim, and they demand that the university hold fast to its traditional roles and character. (And this, too, shall pass!)

Leading in the introduction of change can be both a challenging and a risky proposition. The resistance can be intense and the political backlash threatening. As one who has attempted to illuminate the handwriting on the wall and lead an institution in transforming, I can attest to the lonely, hazardous, and usually frustrating life of a change agent. I am reminded of a quote from Machiavelli: "There is no more delicate matter to take in hand, nor more dangerous to conduct, nor more doubtful of success, than to step up as a leader in the introduction of change. For he who innovates will have for his enemies all those who are well off under the existing order of things, and only lukewarm support in those who might be better off under the new" (Machiavelli, 1950, p. 21). Amen!

It is true that many, both within and outside the academy, believe that significant change must occur not simply in the higher education enterprise as a whole but also in each and every one of our institutions. Most of these individuals see change as an evolutionary, incremental, long-term process, compatible with the values, cultures, and structure of the contemporary college or university.

There are a few voices, however, primarily outside the academy, who believe that both the dramatic nature and compressed time scales that characterize the changes of our times will drive not evolution but revolution. They have serious doubts about whether the challenges of our times will allow such gradual change and adaptation. They point out that there are really no precedents we can draw on. Some even suggest that long before reform of the educational system comes to any conclusion, the system itself will have collapsed (Perelman, 1997).

It is my belief that the forces driving change in higher education, both those from within and those from without, are far more powerful than most realize. It seems likely that both the pace and nature of change in higher education, in America and worldwide, will be considerably beyond what can be accommodated by business-as-usual evolution. As one of my colleagues put it, although there is certainly a good deal of exaggeration and hype about the changes in higher education for the short term (meaning five years or less), it is difficult to stress too strongly the profound nature of the changes that are likely to occur in most of our institutions and in our enterprise over the longer term (a decade and beyond).

The Importance of Experimentation

For the past decade, we have led an effort at the University of Michigan to transform ourselves—to reinvent the institution, if you will, so that it will better serve a rapidly changing world. We strove to create a campus culture in which both excellence and innovation were our highest priorities. We restructured our finances so that we became, in effect, a privately supported public university. We dramatically increased the diversity of our campus community. We launched major efforts to build a modern environment for teaching and research, using the powerful tools of information technology. Yet with each transformative step we took, with every project we launched, we became increasingly uneasy. Change was occurring much more rapidly than we had anticipated.

We concluded that in a world of such rapid and profound change, the most realistic approach was to begin to explore possible futures through experimentation and discovery, to actually build several prototypes of future learning institutions. We have launched or participated as partners in a number of such experiments, aimed at understanding and possibly defining the nature of higher education in the twenty-first century. Let me illustrate with several examples.

Experiment 1: The School of Information

Several years ago, at the University of Michigan, we became so convinced of the potential impact of information technology on the future of our institution that we thought about launching a "skunk works" operation to explore and develop various paradigms for what a twenty-first century university might become. Rather than building an independent research center, we instead decided to take our smallest academic unit, the former School of Library Science, and put at its helm one of our most creative scientists, Dan Atkins, with the challenge of developing new academic programs in "knowledge management." The result has been the rapid evolution—indeed, revolution—of this unit into a new School of Information (see the University of Michigan School of Information Web site at http://www.si.umich.edu/).

Put simply, this school is committed to developing leaders for the information professions who will define, create, and operate facilities and services that will enable users to create, access, and use the information they need. It intends to lead the way in transforming education for the information professions through an innovative curriculum, drawing on the strengths of librarianship, information and computer science, business administration, organizational development, communication, and systems engineering. Its activities range from digital libraries to knowledge networks to virtual educational structures.

Experiment 2: The Media Union

At the University of Michigan we have launched another such experiment to create the type of physical environment that might characterize the future of education: a fascinating new center known as the Media Union (see the Media Union Web site at http://www.ummu.umich.edu/). This is designed to be a laboratory— a test bed—for developing, studying, and perhaps implementing the new paradigms of the university enabled by information technology.

More specifically, this 250,000-square-foot facility, which looks like a modern version of the Temple of Karnak, contains six hundred workstations along with thousands of network jacks for students. The facility contains a one-million-volume science and engineering library, but perhaps more significantly, it is the site of our major digital library projects. There is a sophisticated teleconferencing facility, design studios, visualization laboratories, and a major virtual reality complex with several computer-aided virtual environments. Since art, architecture, and music students work side by side with engineering students, the Media Union contains sophisticated recording studios and electronic music studios. It also has a state-of-the-art soundstage for "digitizing" performances, as well as numerous galleries for displaying the results of student creative efforts. The Media Union is a facility open twenty-four hours a day, seven days a week, primarily designed for students.

Experiment 3: The Michigan Virtual Automotive College

In 1997 we launched a venture known as the Michigan Virtual Automotive College (MVAC) as a private, not-for-profit, 501(c)(3) corporation aimed at developing and delivering technology-enhanced courses and training programs for the automobile industry. The MVAC is a "college without walls" that serves as an interface between higher education institutions, training providers, and the automotive industry. Courses and programs can be offered from literally any site in the state to any other technologically connected site within the state, the United States, or the world. It is expected that the MVAC will broker courses that utilize a wide array of technology platforms, including satellite communications, interactive television, the Internet, CD-ROMs, videotapes, and combinations of these and emerging technologies. It will seek to develop common technology standards among providers and between providers and customers for the ongoing delivery of courses. It currently offers over one hundred courses and training programs, ranging from advanced postgraduate education in engineering, computer technology, and business administration to entry-level instruction in communications, mathematics, and computers.

Based on the success of this first venture, several more industry-specific virtual colleges are being launched through a statewide virtual university. To coordinate these efforts and expand the availability of educational services to the broader public, we are working with state government to design and launch the Michigan Virtual University.

Experiment 4: The Millennium Project

The Millennium Project is a center with the dual missions of studying the forces of change in higher education and exploring possible paradigms for future universities. In some ways, the Millennium Project is an analogue to a corporate R&D laboratory, an incubation center where new paradigms concerning the fundamental missions of the university—teaching, research, service, extension—can be developed and tested (see the Millennium Project Web site at http://milproj.ummu.umich.edu/).

Rather than a "think tank," where ideas are generated and studied, the Millennium Project is a "do tank," where ideas lead to the actual creation of new social forms, which are then available for study. The project draws together scholars and students to develop working models or prototypes to explore possible futures of the university. Like the famous Lockheed Skunk Works, every so often the Millennium Project opens its hanger doors, and something really weird is wheeled out and flown away.

For example, rather than simply exploring the various issues that characterize computer-mediated distance learning, the Millennium Project has instead participated in the development of a virtual or cyberspace university, the Michigan Virtual Automotive College (described previously). Rather than merely examining various elements of international education, the Millennium Project has joined others in an effort to build a truly global university. And rather than simply studying the various social, political, and economic issues swirling about the ever more pervasive use of information technology in our society, the Millennium Project is actually trying to build new types of learning communities in which information technology provides people and their institutions with ubiquitous and robust access to rich knowledge resources and powerful learning opportunities.

A Glimpse of the Future

Clearly, as knowledge and educated people become even more key to prosperity, security, and social well-being, the university, in all its myriad and rapidly changing forms, has become one of the most important social institutions of our times.

Yet many questions remain unanswered. Who will be the learners served by these institutions? Who will teach them? Who will administer and govern these institutions? Who will pay for them? What will be the character of our universities? How will they function? The list goes on.

Perhaps the most profound question of all involves the survival of the university, at least as we know it. Of course, on the one hand, most of us disagree quite strongly with the idea that the university as we know it will cease to exist. On the other hand, I certainly believe there will be forms of the university in the future that we might not recognize from our perspective today.

It is difficult to suggest a particular form for the university of the twenty-first century. The great and ever-increasing diversity that characterizes higher education in America makes it clear that there will be many forms, many types of institutions serving our society. But there are a number of themes that will almost certainly characterize at least some part of the higher education enterprise:

- *A shift from faculty-centered to learner-centered institutions*. The academy will join other social institutions in the public and private sectors in recognizing that we must become more focused on those we serve.

- *Affordability*. Higher education will be within reach of all citizens, whether through lowered costs or societal subsidies.

- *Lifelong learning.* This will reflect both a desire to continue to learn on the part of our citizens and a commitment to provide opportunities for this lifelong learning by our institutions.

- *A seamless web.* All levels of education will not only become interrelated but also will blend together, with learners no longer progressing in lock-step fashion from one level to the next but instead accessing multiple levels of education throughout their lives as their needs change.

- *Asynchronous (anytime, anyplace) learning.* The constraints of time and space will be broken to make learning opportunities more compatible with learners' lifestyles and needs.

- *Interactive and collaborative learning.* Learning approaches will be appropriate for the digital age, the "plug and play" generation.

- *Diversity.* Higher education will serve an increasingly diverse population with diverse needs and goals.

There is one further modifier that may characterize the college or university of the future: *ubiquitous*. Let me explain.

In today's world, knowledge has become the coin of the realm, determining the wealth of nations. It has also become the key to one's personal standard of living, the quality of one's life. We might well make the case that today it has become the responsibility of democratic societies to provide their citizens with the education and training they need throughout their lives, whenever, wherever, and however they desire it, at high quality, and at a cost they can afford.

This has been one of the great themes of higher education in America. Each evolutionary wave of higher education—the public universities, the land-grant universities, the normal and technical colleges, the community colleges—has aimed at educating a broader segment of society. But today we must do even more to serve an even broader segment of our society.

For the past half century, national security was America's most compelling priority, driving major public investments in social institutions such as the research university. Today, however, in the wake of the Cold War and on the brink of the age of knowledge, one could well make the argument that education will replace national defense as the priority of the twenty-first century. Perhaps this will become the new social contract that will determine the character of our educational institutions, just as the government-university research partnership did in the latter half of the twentieth century. We might even conjecture that a social contract based on developing the abilities and talents of our people to their fullest extent could well transform our schools, colleges, and universities into new forms that will rival the research university in importance.

Once again we need a new paradigm for delivering the opportunity for learning to even broader segments of our society. Fortunately, today's technology is rapidly breaking the constraints of space and time. It has become clear that most people, in most areas, can learn—and learn well—using asynchronous learning (that is, "anytime, anyplace, anywhere" education). Modern information technology has largely cut us free from the constraints of space and time and has freed our educational system from these constraints as well. The barriers are no longer cost or technology but perception and habit. Lifetime education is rapidly becoming a reality, making learning available for anyone who wants to learn, at the time and place of their choice, without great personal effort or cost.

But this may not be enough. Instead of asynchronous learning, perhaps we should instead consider a future of "ubiquitous learning"—learning for everyone, in every place, all the time. Indeed, in a world driven by an ever-expanding knowledge base, continuous learning, like continuous improvement, has become a necessity of life.

Rather than an "age of knowledge," could we instead aspire to a "culture of learning," in which people are continually surrounded by, immersed in, and absorbed in learning experiences? Information technology has now provided us with the means to create learning environments throughout one's life. Not only are these environments able to transcend the constraints of space and time; they, like us, are capable of learning and evolving to serve our changing educational needs. This may become not only the great challenge but the compelling vision facing higher education as it enters the next millennium.

References

Breneman, D. W., Finney, J. E., and Roherty, B. M. *Shaping the Future: Higher Education Finance in the 1990s*. San Jose: California Higher Education Policy Center, 1997.

Dionne, J. L., and Kean, T. *Breaking the Social Contract: The Fiscal Crisis in Higher Education*. (Report of the Commission on National Investment in Higher Education.) New York: Council for Aid to Education, 1997.

Machiavelli, N. *The Prince*. New York: Random House, 1950.

Perelman, L. "Barnstorming with Lewis Perelman." *Educom Review*, 1997, 32(2), 18–26.

2

Competitive Strategies for Higher Education in the Information Age

Richard N. Katz

Traditional revenue sources for U.S. higher education are, and will continue to be, under downward pressure. When faced with such pressure, colleges and universities have a limited set of responses. They can cut costs (with or without cutting quality), raise prices, exit existing markets, pursue new markets, create new products, or pursue any combination of these strategies.

A few institutions have pursued aggressively a set of academic strategies designed to extend the reach of their instructional offerings geographically or to offer for sale new or repackaged products in different markets. Many colleges and universities are only now engaging in structured dialogue about how emerging information technologies may be employed to enable such strategies.

This chapter identifies an important revenue opportunity for (or threat to) U.S. higher education, identifies strategies for exploiting this opportunity, and raises potential policy issues associated with it. The perspective offered here is unabashedly economic and entrepreneurial. At the same time, my premises honor the fact that colleges and universities are not businesses in the ordinary sense, and I am mindful of the fact that important issues of public policy are overlooked in pursuing an economic perspective. Some of the ideas reflected in the discussion will cut against higher education's cultural grain. The corresponding hope is that the business case for action is sufficiently compelling to stimulate serious dialogue in the academy about an area of growing importance.

How Postsecondary Education May Change

Following are seven assumptions about how postsecondary instruction and the delivery and consumption of academic information may change in the next decade. These assumptions do not portend the demise of the classical classroom model of instructional delivery but rather the enrichment and diversification of this model through the incorporation of emerging technologies. The central assumptions are that in the next decade

1. Ubiquitous, high-speed, economically accessible network capacity will exist nationally and, to a great extent, globally.

2. Affordable, multimedia-capable computers will be commonplace, and most leading universities will assume student ownership of such devices.

3. U.S. graduate education is and will continue to be a major export industry. Colleges and universities that enjoy great reputations can and will attract student bodies regionally, nationally, and even globally. The creative application of instructional innovation and advanced technology will open the door to less well known providers of postsecondary education, including those in private industry. Technical sophistication and price may permit significant "leapfrogging" in this emerging market.

4. Most colleges and universities will deliver some portion of their instructional offerings via communication networks. As these networks create the potential for global university outreach across significant elements of higher education's mission, course content and intellectual property holdings will become scarce economic goods and will command an economic premium.

5. As the ability to use technology in support of instruction improves, the differentiators of technology-enriched course offer-

ings will continue to be price, quality, and access. Institutions (or corporations) that succeed in delivering instruction in a networked fashion will need to move well beyond the educational-TV model of "talking heads" and leverage faculty reputations and unique information repositories. The ability to deliver instruction in ways that meet students' geographical and scheduling needs will become increasingly important.

6. Nontraditional sources of university-caliber instruction, such as software developers and publishers, are likely to become increasingly important suppliers of course content and materials in select and highly remunerative educational niches (for example, corporate training). The employment relationships between academic institutions and their faculty will become even more complex, as publishers and software firms contract with career-ladder professors to create, develop, and deliver courseware under private arrangements. Interactive multimedia will demand ongoing faculty participation (including "virtual office hours") and will blur many of the existing distinctions between college and university investments in course materials and investments made by commercial publishers. The ability of colleges and universities to recover (at least) the indirect costs of their support of courseware development and delivery will become a significant issue.

7. Within this time frame, the laws that govern intellectual property will change significantly. In particular, the application of publisher-preferred protections to the digital distribution of copyrighted materials is likely to have enormous revenue and expense implications for higher education in general and for technology-enriched instruction in particular. The legal and economic management of university intellectual property will become a complex area of activity. Within higher education, these changes—and campus responses—will create new winners and losers in the "balance of trade" in intellectual property. Depending on how this legal environment and the resultant competition evolve, higher education as a whole may win or lose vis-à-vis other intellectual

content creators and distributors (Information Infrastructure Task Force, 1995).

Although bold, the preceding assumptions are defensible. Regarding network services, growth in use of the Internet and the World Wide Web have exceeded 20 percent per month for several years. Major investments by the Library of Congress, the National Science Foundation, and others in digital libraries will accelerate network acceptance and usage. Importantly, non-higher-education use of the Internet and its resources is now growing at a rate exceeding the rate within higher education.

Trends in personal computer pricing and performance continue to outstrip even the rosiest industry forecasts. It is certainly reasonable to assume that network-ready and video-capable workstations will be commonly available for less than $2,000. In addition, so-called network computers and sub-$1,000 personal computers are placing networked information within the economic reach of anyone with access to a wide-area network, including many of the domestic rural areas and developing nations that have been underserved by higher education.

As regards revenue potential, U.S. higher education, in all facets of its activities, is a $180–billion-per-year industry. Although enrollments are rising nationally for graduates and undergraduates, many higher education sources of revenue are diminishing. Total revenue growth for most segments of higher education is likely to slow in the decade ahead, as compared with growth rates in the 1980s. In this context, educational leaders will have to choose among low-growth strategies such as cost containment and capitated enrollments, erosion of program quality, or revenue-enhancing revisions to their institutions' missions. The "infotainment" industry, which includes television, telecommunications, print media, entertainment, and other segments, will soon be a $1–trillion-per-year industry. The segments of this industry that produce and manage information content will account for more than $550 billion in annual sales, and revenues in this segment will grow at 15 to 20 percent annually.

In sum, the most economically robust opportunities for postsecondary instruction and distribution of primary source materials may lie outside U.S. higher education's primary delivery mechanisms and markets. New information technologies and trends in the infotainment marketplace will make it possible to bring U.S. colleges and universities into classrooms, and even living rooms, around the globe.

This opportunity carries with it tremendous implications related to the role and missions of many academic institutions and regarding the nature and meaning of access to a higher education experience. Some of these policy implications include

- A need to rethink the ownership of faculty course materials and the incentive system for faculty participation in courseware production

- The potential for, and meaning of, "franchising" a campus's course materials and intellectual property

- New educational roles for educators in the K–12 arena

- The possible redefining or blurring of roles between different segments of higher education (research institutions, comprehensive institutions, community colleges, and so on) and between higher education and K–12 education

- New ways to reach and educate other higher education constituents, such as farmers, ranchers, doctors, lawyers, and others whose learning needs are specialized and lifelong

- A greater focus on accreditation and the assessment of learning outcomes

Finally, participation in this new delivery approach to instruction is both risky and exciting and will require both early strategy setting and institutional planning and investment. In particular, at the microeconomic level, to realize the academic and economic potential embodied by this opportunity, colleges and universities must begin now to determine how to differentiate their instructional offerings from those of others in higher education or industry. At the macroeconomic level, the application of information technology to the distribution of postsecondary instruction is not necessarily a zero-sum game. As an industry, U.S. higher education should explore how to leverage the global preeminence of U.S. colleges and universities in ways that can increase total revenues. Importantly, success in increasing such revenues will make it possible for institutions to support traditional modes of instruction and to subsidize important but nonremunerative areas of campus life.

Information Technology at the End of the Twentieth Century

In a 1995 speech, Vice President Al Gore stated, "The new marketplace will no longer be divided along current sectoral lines. There may not be cable companies or phone companies or computer companies, as such. Everyone will be in the bit business. The functions provided will define the marketplace. There will be information conduits, information providers, information appliances, and information consumers." Gore's bold but widely accepted vision raises the question of what role, if any, U.S. higher education will choose to assume in this evolving marketplace. After all, universities are both important providers *and* consumers of information, and the evolution of the mass market for information technology will not leave such institutions unscathed.

To frame such a discussion, it is necessary first for colleges and universities to establish some general planning assumptions about information technology and to incorporate thinking about such assumptions into their missions and plans for delivering instruction. Information technology–intensive companies place the utmost importance on this kind of strategic thinking and, in many cases, have defined visions of the future that might surprise many in higher education. For example, according to Oracle chief executive Larry Ellison, "the goal of the great Library of Alexandria was nothing less than to collect all of the histories, all of the science, all of the philosophy that had ever been written—the collective knowledge of mankind. That's what this is going to be: all of the text, all of the image data, all of the tabular information, all of the audio, all of the video . . . will be stored for you [electronically] to call up and review" (Allen, Ebeling, and Scott, 1995, p. 31). Such a vision has tremendous implications for higher education.

Convergence

The most important phenomenon in the evolving information technology marketplace is referred to as convergence. Convergence is the "accelerating trend of companies involved in broadcasting, cable television, computers, entertainment, and retailing businesses to form various combinations in order to gain competitive advantage in the huge new info-tainment market" (Allen, Ebeling, and Scott, 1995).

The demise of both anti–vertical integration consent decrees in the motion picture industry and financial syndication ("fin-syn") limitations on broadcast television—and more recently the passage of the Telecommunications Act of 1996—has paved the way for the creation, by merger or alliance, of monolithic information conglomerates. These legal changes make it possible for information developers to also own elements of the information distribution channels or retail outlets delivering their product. The mergers and alliance-building activity taking place now is strategic in nature and is designed to align information creation (production), communications (distribution), and retail selling (the "set-top box"). Control of both production and distribution has, since the 1920s, been discouraged due to the risk of fostering monopolistic practices. This risk of monopoly underlies the Justice Department's recent concern with Microsoft's Web browser. In this kind of competitive environment, colleges, universities, and other suppliers of instructional "products" will have to view the choice of information distributors as a strategic one, just as motion picture production companies have been strategically selective about their distributors.

Assumptions About Technology

The rush to merge, join, or enter a variety of joint ventures is based on a number of shared assumptions about the nature of evolving information technologies and about the mass market for interactive multimedia. There is general support for these assumptions across a number of firms and industries that will compete in this marketplace. Some of the most important planning assumptions include the following:

- The "converged" forces arrayed to support the delivery of interactive multimedia to the home will approach $1 trillion (1993 constant dollars) in annual sales by the late 1990s.

- Organizations that produce "information content" will generate annual revenues of $550 to $600 billion, which will grow 15 to 20 percent annually. These organizations include film producers, software developers, publishers, and others.

- The most popular network service offerings will be movies on demand, home shopping, video games, instructional programs, participatory television, and remote banking.

- By the year 2000, switched broadband services will penetrate at least 40 percent of the residential and small business markets across the United States.

- Information (that is, educational) applications may be at least as important as entertainment in this evolving market.

- The most formidable competitors are expected to be strategic partnerships—especially between content providers and controllers of distribution channels. Among industry leaders, the key attributes for success are thought to be clear management vision, creative marketing, a risk-taking culture, and the right strategic relationships.

- Of the different stages of the infotainment value chain, control over information content has the highest relative importance.

- The requisite enabling technologies are available now. Therefore, the critical issues are business and regulatory issues, not technology issues. For U.S. higher education, the issues are predominantly cultural, including those related to risk aversion, urgency, and the ability to assimilate change.

- Recent surveys confirm a strong interest in distance learning and related student services for residential use.

What prudent conclusions, then, can be drawn about this "convergence" from these planning assumptions?

First, it seems fair to conclude that both market forces and technology are converging to deliver many new capabilities in the very near future. Higher education, as both a major supplier and consumer of information resources, can neither sit this dance out nor wait to be asked. Inaction is making it possible, for example, for a variety of new and traditional educators to compete for students' time and allegiance in areas of high academic demand. The possible loss, to new competitors, of enrollments in areas like business or psychology will place new pressures on institutions with comprehensive curricula. In effect, new competition, enabled by information technology, will "cherry pick" those offerings that subsidize much of the academy.

Second, higher education—as a content producer—occupies the most potentially profitable niche in this convergence and is the producer of choice identified in many surveys of consumer preference.

Third, based on the potential for profit, newcomers are likely to be attracted to the business of selling courses electronically. The advantages that higher education enjoys in both accreditation and reputation may be tenuous (in some educational markets) when private industry suppliers weigh in with bigger budgets, better technology, more competitive institutional cultures, and more comfort with managing strategic alliances.

Competition in a Technology-Enriched Context

Although colleges and universities rarely express their policies, intentions, and practices in competitive terms, the pressure on traditional resources, coupled with the emergence of technology-based education delivery systems, will force competitive thinking. One particularly interesting case of the assimilation of certain business values in the higher education context is the University of Phoenix (UOP), which focuses on the educational needs of working adults. UOP is an accredited, degree-granting institution and is a subsidiary of the Apollo Group, a publicly traded corporation. UOP's growth in revenues exceeds that of the higher education industry as a whole, by a considerable amount.

Several of the assumptions referred to previously will drive the need for competitive and strategic thinking in higher education. The primary drivers of a changed outlook include the following:

- Educational applications will be remunerative in the infotainment market.

- The size and growth attributes of this market are likely to attract new and nontraditional competitors.

- Innovative and entrepreneurial colleges and universities will enter into unusual alliances with nontraditional partners.

- The failure to innovate and invest relatively early will foreclose competitive options for many colleges and universities.

- Colleges and universities with the most intellectual capital will have a new and powerful source of competitive advantage.

The early signs of the changing rules of competition are already in evidence. An independent for-profit corporation called the Home Education Network has acquired the right to distribute the content of UCLA Extension's courses via CD-ROM, online services, and direct broadcast satellite. Motorola University contracts with colleges and universities around the world to develop and deliver a curriculum to Motorola Corporation employees. Elsevier Publishing is working with universities to deliver the full text of its materials science journals over the Internet. Microsoft Corporation is working with many colleges and universities to license the distribution and sale of these institutions' library holdings. Finally, as the price-performance ratio of important technologies, particularly network-based video, continues to improve, nearly every U.S. university will engage in offering "distance education." In such a context, competitive advantage will not follow simply because one delivers education this way. Importantly, competitive advantage will accrue to those who deliver such education cheaper, better, or in a more targeted fashion (Porter, 1980, p. 39).

The Marketeer and the Academy

The very idea of marketing seems antithetical, to some, to the mission, values, and ideals of the academic community. The term, if not the concept, is avoided in favor of more noble ones such as *development, recruitment,* and *outreach.* Curriculum development, often the exclusive purview of the faculty, is an activity conducted with only secondary consideration given to market factors. Once students have matriculated, their choices are circumscribed by campus resource constraints, faculty schedules, and the underlying philosophy of *in loco parentis.* These forces are compounded by the fact that, at many of our institutions, faculty bereft of the gift of teaching are, for a variety of reasons, "sentenced" with their students to the classroom. This conspiracy of factors accounts for a portion of every campus's student attrition and is structurally unsuited to the likely competitive market for technology-enriched instruction.

A more likely structural and behavioral model is found in the context of university extension operations. Many university extension operations and other academic institutions that cater to the needs of the working adult student have developed values, business systems, and capabilities that will be required in this new context:

- Each class produces marginal revenue, at a marginal cost.

- Instructional contribution can be (and usually is) a variable cost.

- Different courses have different appeal in different markets.

- Advertising can influence student choice.

- Close study of market demand allows the development of curricula that can either maximize earnings or fulfill noneconomic policy objectives.

- Unsuitable instructors are not "invited" back.

- Big name faculty attract students.

- Location and scheduling decisions have revenue implications and are treated as market factors for curriculum
  and program planning purposes.

I offer this characterization of the cultural, behavioral, and business attributes of a "market-sensitive" academic institution not for
the purpose of advocacy but to accent the fact that the needs of resident students and distant students are likely to be markedly different. Further, it is almost axiomatic that the network-based
consumer of higher education intellectual content will be peri-
patetic in the extreme and, eventually, will have unprecedented
choice in course offerings and institutional affiliations. In the net-
work-mediated context, physical location, student events, or other
traditional factors will not likely influence loyalty to an institution.
In this context, capabilities like market-influenced curricular planning, technical sophistication, advertising, and instructional quality control will be necessary elements of the instructional delivery
system. Institutions that choose to follow this path must assess the
compatibility of such value systems, competencies, and business systems with their existing academic cultures and business systems.

Of all the competencies and values that must accompany an
institutional decision to pursue opportunities in the delivery of technologically enriched instruction, probably none is as important as
the ability to differentiate among the size, dimensions, and other
attributes of various academic market niches. For example, many
analysts suggest that the market for lifelong learning is larger (and
is growing faster) than the degree-granting segment (Davis and
Botkin, 1994). If, following this example, much of the market
growth (that is, public demand) for postsecondary education is to
occur outside the traditional residential undergraduate context,
institutions must be prepared to assess what serving such different
markets might mean for the faculty as well as for the residential student body, and what requirements such service will place on the
business systems of the campus. For example, business systems that

assume that students will stand in line to register for classes are unlikely to meet the needs of the distant learner.

These needs are not likely to be met, in the long term, by a traditional course catalog, a traditional registrar, and a traditional admissions process. The consumer of geography-independent instructional offerings and information resources may—in his or her worst manifestation—be an educational "channel surfer," scouring the Internet and World Wide Web for timely, relevant, and well-priced courses. Such an individual will likely expect more than a short narrative description, will assume that registration and payment can occur online, and will expect online digital library privileges and a host of other services mediated over the network. Colleges and universities will want this individual to know about ancillary products that are available: related video and audio programs, online tutorials and books, and so forth. In all, the support environment for a college or university curriculum delivered over a network will require much greater integration and sophistication than does the counterpart support environment offered on campus. Raising the integration standard for off-campus offerings will, in turn, raise the expectations of resident students and the campus's capacity to meet these expectations.

A market-sensitive, planning-based approach will be important to the campus's decisions about whether to pursue certain opportunities and will consider what the possible financial implications of such decisions are likely to be. The market plan will be at least three-dimensional and should address

- The product (both the discipline and the delivery medium)

- The market (resident learners? distant learners? degree-program learners? non–degree program learners?)

- The geographical focus (campus? local? regional? national? global?)

Although this three-dimensional model greatly oversimplifies the market planning process that information-age educators should consider, it does introduce the choice of instructional technology into curricular planning and decision making. Curriculum planning in a place-bound (that is, campus) context is framed by the questions of curricular need, faculty availability, enrollment size, enrollment demand, and classroom size and availability. In the context of technology-enriched teaching and learning, the number of planning variables expands to include choices of instructional technology, market geography, customer attributes, and time. Asynchronous-learning technologies such as instruction via CD or broadcast or taped video or audio can actually mitigate the constraint of faculty availability, whereas synchronous-learning technologies (such as online "global" office hours) offer possibilities for customizing and personalizing instruction in ways that will likely increase the demand for faculty.

As Figure 2.1 indicates, campuses that choose to extend their instructional reach with the use of technology have many competitive options. For example, what is the demand for a technology-enriched Ivy League MBA curriculum in Russia? What might the market be for university-developed practical agricultural course material on cassette? What elements of U.S. corporations' training needs can be met by U.S. higher education and by any campus in particular—and in what format or medium? What is the educational role of credentialing and certification in this environment?

If this wealth of capabilities, markets, and intellectual capital represents an untapped opportunity for U.S. colleges and universities in the emerging marketplace, the realization of this opportunity depends on: faculty vision and business execution; the creation of, and investment in, new academic and business strategies; creative marketing; risk taking; and the development of strategic relationships. Absent early institutional intervention in establishing a framework for exploiting this opportunity, colleges and universities run the risk of

- Diluting our intellectual resources through the willy-nilly application of network technologies to the instructional delivery system

- Dissipating our intellectual resources through unregulated deal making between individual faculty and their "electronic" publishers

- Cheapening our intellectual resources by failing to ensure that technology-enriched course offerings are, in fact, enriched relative to traditional offerings

- Draining our intellectual resources by trying to cover every product market niche in the absence of an overall strategy

- Abdicating a potential leadership role in this emerging market to new competitors such as Times-Mirror, Microsoft, or Oracle

It should be noted that those who do not produce course content in this marketplace are likely to become consumers of others' content.

Expanding U.S. Higher Education's Instructional Franchise

The objective of this chapter is to organize information about the environmental context in which higher education may operate in the near future and to raise questions about how such contextual observations may be translated by the higher education industry and individual institutions into new strategic directions and programs. For this reason, this discussion is long on themes and short on recommendations. If the underlying premise that the convergence of technologies will enable new ways to fulfill higher education's teaching mission is true, then leading institutions have a range of strategic options that can expand both their geographical instructional

Figure 2.1. Product-Market Segmentation Chart.

Education Media/Products

Education Markets	Traditional (classroom based)	Educational TV	Multisite Video	Electronic Faculty Office Hours	Audiocassette	Self-Contained Educational Technology	Information Resources on Demand CD/Network	Full Interactive Multimedia
Undergraduate Degree								
Graduate Degree								
Professional Degree								
Continuing Education								
Executive Education								
Agricultural Education								
Corporate Training								
Campus Training								
ESL, Continuing Legal, Medical								
Intersegmental Education/K-12								

reach and their sources of revenues. This range of options extends from achieving cost efficiencies by leveraging course offerings among existing university students to seeking new, potentially global, markets by franchising courses and information assets to students not currently served by higher education.

The first and primary recommendation is for our educational leadership to *develop strategic frameworks for addressing the changing environment that is described here*. Any institution's ability to exploit new instructional opportunities effectively depends on its establishing an *institutional* context for program development and institutional investments to "jump start" such development. Although U.S. colleges and universities are prepared, for example, to create the data communications networks that will carry instructional content and information resources, is it appropriate (to their missions) for these institutions to "seed" the development of best-in-their-class technology-enriched instructional offerings? Many of our institutions have achieved academic recognition and excellence by localizing the responsibilities for curriculum development and execution as deeply as possible. The development of truly enriched, technology-intensive course offerings—worthy of the reputation of U.S. higher education—will be costly and risky. The governance and organizational infrastructures for making such investment decisions are not well developed currently.

A strategic framework must also *address the very sensitive issue of who owns the rights—for distribution and sale purposes—to institutions' instructional materials and collections*. In this area, the nature of the new technologies and the need for unprecedented investments will change or challenge the traditional model wherein faculty course notes belong exclusively to their authors. In the extreme case of fully franchised multimedia course productions, course notes may become more analogous to theatrical scripts, and faculty roles may become analogous, variously, to those of scriptwriters, producers, directors, and "stars." The evolving roles created by the new potential to "export" course materials beyond the campus suggest the need for new thinking about property rights, risk sharing, royalties, residuals, and other cost-sharing and compensation strategies. What might it mean, for example, in cultural, ethical, and legal terms, for one institution's faculty member to contract with another party to produce a multimedia course (including electronic office hours) for distribution—for use in credit-granting courses—to other universities? Many of the possibilities created by new approaches to delivering instruction are *not* natural extensions of the traditional relationships between faculty, their home campuses, and their publishers.

The implementation of distance education within U.S. higher education should force us to *rethink the issues surrounding the awarding of campus credit*. The deployment of instruction beyond the borders of a campus should foster (or force) a national dialogue about the interchangeability of credits among participating institutions. If, for example, a student enrolled at one institution enrolls in an electronic course "produced" by another and completes successfully the exams and papers necessary for the award of course credit at the producing campus, can this student be awarded course credit at the "home" institution? If the answer is no, then the speed of adoption of new delivery approaches is likely to be retarded, and instructional innovations are likely to occur first in private industry, where increasing numbers of unusual providers will seek and receive degree-granting accreditation. If the answer is yes, then many approaches to offering technology-enriched instruction have the potential to alter fundamentally the nature and meaning of our student bodies and faculties, to each other and to our institutions.

A strategic framework should *focus simultaneously on the issues of public policy, institutional priorities and identity, and business*. Beginning with a product-market segmentation, as represented in Figure 2.1, the nation's higher education leadership should address the issues of how technologically enriched course offerings affect institutional image, access, quality, and cost as well as the question of whether or not (and how big!) a market exists for new instructional offerings. For example, the creation of courses under the auspices of many universities' schools of business and engineering may have significant revenue potential in the executive education and staff training markets. Clearly, the potential geographical market for such courses is global. (For example, one top-twenty graduate school of management is considering a corporate technology partnership to deliver the MBA curriculum via distance learning technologies to a major Third World nation.) On the one hand, in this market segment the revenue potentials are high, whereas the negative public policy impacts are likely to be negligible. On the other hand, a decision to develop a best-in-its-class multimedia course on world civilization may have lower revenue potentials but significant potential in the public policy arena. Such course programming—and the associated investments—could raise the standard of instruction in key areas, but it also carries with it the risks of "homogenizing" course content and reducing instructional and intellectual diversity.

Whatever the institutional and public policy implications, it is clear that demand for remote instruction in a variety of postsecondary disciplines exists. The key questions for policymakers are

- Whether or not to get involved.

- What it may mean—pedagogically, culturally, and economically—to get involved.

- Whether or not noninvolvement is sustainable. (Deciding to be a consumer of others' intellectual content is as consequential as deciding to become a supplier of content.)

The strategic planning exercise should also *address the issue of technology risk*. This discussion has been long on optimism concerning the potential of new educational technologies and short on assessment of the risks of such technologies. Those who were involved in higher education's early euphoria over the transformational potential of educational television are especially mindful of the risks of overselling new technology. It is clear that the full potential for registering students electronically, receiving funds electronically, exchanging transcript information electronically, delivering enriching multimedia courses, transmitting test scores and grade reports electronically, and keeping electronic records of all registered students cannot be realized with today's technology. If an institution's strategy in this area embraces this kind of target environment, the development of the strategic framework should include an assessment of the underlying technology requirements of such an environment and a forecast of when needed technologies will be available commercially.

Finally, *a strategic framework should address the institutional policy concerning the formation of new strategic partnerships and acknowledge their operational and economic implications*. A discussion of strategy should include an assessment of the institution's capabilities across the media production value chain and should identify the kinds of partners that will be needed to maximize the opportunity and minimize the risks of early adoption of a technological approach. Grant opportunities for early test cases should be explored.

Summary

In sum, technology will, in the intermediate term, be the least important determinant of success in the new delivery of postsecondary instructional offerings. The determinant of market success in this arena will continue to be the quality of the intellectual content. Although intellectual content will be king as this market evolves, short-term advantages will accrue to those who move first into this market, as there are many consumers who will sacrifice perceived quality in favor of course offerings that address their lifestyle needs (time and distance) more closely. This likelihood, in concert with the fact that elite institutions may view themselves as having more to lose in reputational terms than they have to gain, may allow the more visionary and less conservative institutions to dominate certain instructional niches. The conservatism and consensual governance model characteristic of higher education institutions, collectively, may make it possible for the earliest adopters to come from private industry. The public policy ramifications of the private industry alternative are enormous.

U.S. higher education is the envy of the world. Our faculty, facilities, and holdings are sought after beyond the traditional reaches of our campuses. New information technologies will make it possible for this reach to extend well beyond the ivory tower. Significant demand for higher education—on an anytime, anyplace basis—exists and will grow as the creative application of these technologies to teaching and learning matures. The application of new technologies to postsecondary education creates a significant likelihood that new players—those without fixed investments in physical plants or tenured professors—will obtain accreditation and will compete with traditional colleges and universities in a number of markets. In particular, technology firms will likely attempt to leverage their networks and technology bases to produce highly sophisticated courses at lower costs than can colleges and universities that need to amortize "bricks and mortar" across their offerings. In many cases, instructional offerings from private firms will be produced, prepared, and delivered by our faculty—who may be paid royalties based on the size of the "gate." This possibility has the potential to change U.S. higher education in profound ways.

For these reasons, U.S. colleges and universities must overcome the natural conservatism of their faculties regarding this opportunity. The potential exists to produce new revenues through technology-enriched extensions of our instructional programs. These new revenues can reinforce the traditional, campus-based instructional environments we have created with much success. The role of the college or university as a center of culture, a community of scholars, and a physical place is secure. The mission of the college or university is also secure. The global need and demand for higher learning is growing. Thoughtfully applied, new information technologies will make economically possible a new level of investment in collegiate instruction. Such investment can sustain our collective vigor and excellence—if we can rise to the challenge.

References

Allen, D., Ebeling, H. W., and Scott, L. "Perspectives on the Convergence of Communications, Information, Retailing, and Entertainment: Speeding Toward the Interactive Multimedia Age." Unpublished company report, Deloitte & Touche, 1995.

Davis, S., and Botkin, J. *The Monster Under the Bed: How Business Is Mastering the Opportunity of Knowledge for Profit.* New York: Simon & Schuster, 1994.

Information Infrastructure Task Force. *Intellectual Property and the National Information Infrastructure: Report of the Working Group on Intellectual Property Rights.* Washington, D.C.: U.S. Government Printing Office, 1995.

Porter, M. *Competitive Strategy.* Old Tappan, N.J.: Macmillan, 1980.

3

Assessing the New Competitive Landscape

Harvey Blustain, Philip Goldstein, Gregory Lozier

Higher education institutions are voicing concern over new competition in their industry. But does "new competition" denote colleges' and universities' moving into new geographical markets and encountering established local institutions? Does it mean new delivery mechanisms (for example, Web-based virtual education) that threaten to supplant traditional pedagogical techniques? Does it refer to the development of corporate universities? Or does it refer to the fact that for-profit educational institutions are now a $3.5-billion-a-year business and growing at more than 10 percent a year?

The short answer is yes.

Colleges and universities are being assaulted from several directions with new competitors, new technologies, and new approaches to education. Many have chosen to ignore the warning signs, hoping it will all just go away. Others have rolled out a few online courses or have encouraged deans to develop new programs. Few institutions have developed a coherent strategy for ensuring success in the new environment.

Our fundamental contention here is that fainthearted attempts to test the waters will not hold back the tide of nontraditional competition. A complex array of forces—new delivery technologies, changing demographics, the emergence of corporate universities, and a complex global economy—is creating a new competitive landscape, and institutions must think methodically about how they want to respond. In this chapter, we present a framework for beginning to do just that.

After reviewing the drivers and trends within higher education, we turn to the sources of competitive advantage in the new marketplace and relate them to specific market segments. Following a brief case study, we discuss how to develop an institutional strategy to capitalize on the new marketplace opportunities.

The Drivers of Education

A good place to begin the analytical framework is with the learner. Why do people seek educational opportunities? What are they looking for? What drives their desire for education?

For much of this century, higher education was an opportunity for a privileged minority of eighteen- to twenty-two-year-olds to gain some knowledge and acquire skills. Today, the motivations are more complex. In addition to providing young people with a venue for growing up, colleges and universities are increasingly providing services to adult learners and corporations, creating additional factors driving the market for advanced education. Consequently, higher education's mission has expanded to include the following goals:

- *Provide knowledge to the workforce.* Capitalism's "creative destruction" produces an unending stream of new markets, products, services, and technologies, all of which demand training. Businesses spend untold billions of dollars on educating their workforce, and many corporations have established their own universities, often in partnership with traditional colleges and universities.

- *Retool people for new careers.* Conventional wisdom suggests that people will change careers several times in their lifetime. Some of the retooling will come through on-the-job training, but an increasing amount is coming through targeted programs that meet the needs of selective adult consumers. Education has often been described as recession-proof, since people out of work frequently go back to school to reboot their careers.

- *Cater to the need for mental stimulation.* The desire for self-improvement has deep roots in American culture. From matchbook courses to self-help books, from motivational seminars to elder hostels, technology and leisure have enabled a burgeoning market for education for education's sake.

Even among the traditional college set, expectations about the value of education have changed. A recent survey of 350,000 students at 665 institutions, sponsored by the American Council on Education, showed that 75 percent considered financial success to be a very important goal of education, compared with 41 percent who believed education could provide them with a meaningful philosophy of life. This was a reversal of the motivations found among students thirty years earlier. If worldly success is an important driver for education, colleges and universities in a competitive environment may need to pay attention to what their customers want rather than to what others think they need.

Environmental Trends

The expansion in drivers of education has been accompanied by changes in the social environment, all of which, cumulatively, signal increased competition for colleges and universities. The major changes include

- *Demographics.* Many people in higher education look comfortingly at the "baby boom echo" that began to inject a surge of college-age students into the pipeline in 1994 and will continue for some thirty

years. However, the second half of this era will also
be the period when baby boomers retire and will place
greater demands on public funds for Social Security
and Medicare. Can institutions (especially public institutions) count on resources being available for expansion during this period? Or will private colleges—and
for-profit providers—have to pick up the slack?

- *Technology.* Considerable ink and blood have already
been shed about the application of technology to education. Those who still question its appropriateness,
however, should recall President Rutherford B. Hayes's
comment on seeing a demonstration of the telephone
in 1876: "That's an amazing invention, but who would
ever want to use one of them?"

- *The overcoming of time and space.* In a world of twenty-
four-hour financial markets, real-time global video
games, telecommuting, and instant images from Mars,
there is no reason why pedagogy must depend on
rounding up students into one room for fifty minutes,
three times a week.

- *An "800 number, ATM" mentality.* When students can
get cash at 2 A.M., download library materials at 3 A.M.,
and order shoes from L. L. Bean at 4 A.M., it is only
educational inertia that keeps them convinced that
they must learn calculus by sitting in the same classroom for fifty minutes, three times a week.

- *Blurring of industry boundaries.* The health care and
insurance industries, once distinct, have merged. The
computer, consumer electronics, telecommunications,
and entertainment industries have evolved into an
amalgamated digital industry. Colleges and universities
cannot continue to draw boundaries around themselves

and say, "We are the only legitimate players in the higher education business."

- *Proliferation of authority figures.* Professors used to be the accepted authority on virtually any subject. But in America today, journalists, think tank gurus, movie stars, and businesspeople speak with equal authority. Whatever pre-eminence the professoriate once enjoyed in public debate has been eroded by the omnipresence of anyone with an opinion and a talk show.

- *The individual as the business unit.* The social contract between employers and employees has changed, and there is no longer an expectation of lifetime (or even long-term) employment. Savvy employees keep their skills current, and this has turned many people into discriminating buyers of educational services.

All of these trends have served to alter the competitive landscape within higher education. Consumers of education have new motivations and expectations, technology is challenging medieval pedagogical methods, public perceptions of education have become more democratic, and for-profit corporations have realized the wealth of a new market opportunity. The ivory tower is under siege.

Sources of Competitive Advantage

One element that frames any institution's marketing strategy is the needs of buyers. When the "customer" is an eighteen-year-old freshman seeking a good education, the sources of competitive advantage are relatively easy to define:

- *Reputation.* Is this a good school? Will potential employers want to see this school on my resume? What does my neighbor who goes there say about it?

- *Curriculum and educational standards.* Does it offer the program I want in electrical engineering? Will it prepare me for my career? Can I get in?

- *Cost.* Can I afford to go there? Can I get a scholarship or a loan? What kind of discount can I negotiate?

- *Location.* Is it near my home? Is it far away from my parents? Will it give me the urban (or rural or suburban) experience I want?

- *Student activities.* Does the school have a good athletic program? a debate team? fraternities?

Adult learners and corporations bring different sets of expectations to the marketplace, and therefore they create new sources of competitive advantage for colleges and universities:

- *Access.* Because adults and businesspeople are not looking for a residential experience, convenient schedules and proximity to work and home become prime differentiators.

- *Partnerships.* Corporations are looking for partners with whom it is easy to do business. Having to go through numerous faculty committees before new courses are developed or instructors are appointed may diminish an institution's perceived responsiveness and value.

- *Customized curriculum.* Corporations often outsource education so that they can receive the latest training in skills, technology, or practices. For example, in response to external pressures, a financial services business might ask for the rapid development of an "Ethical Considerations in Derivatives Trading" course.

- *Flexible delivery*. A corporation might ask for instruction to be delivered in New York, Frankfurt, Hong Kong, and Sao Paolo within two months. The institution that says, "Yeah, we can do that" will win in the new marketplace.

- *Use of technology*. Adults have limited patience with a "talking head" instructional style. Accustomed to a higher standard of technology usage, corporate customers see technological sophistication as an important differentiator among providers.

The issue, therefore, goes beyond questions such as "Do we want to enter the market, and if so, what do we offer?" To be effective in this market may require a fundamental reorientation in how the institution does business: how it relates to students, works with partners, and manages its internal processes.

Market Segment Characteristics

Traditional and nontraditional markets have different growth potential and profitability characteristics. They offer various opportunities for nontraditional players, and similarly, current players are threatened differentially.

The traditional market segment includes undergraduate students, graduate professionals, and graduate arts and sciences students.

1. *Undergraduate market*. Tied closely to demography, the traditional undergraduate market will experience some growth over the ensuing decades. However, competition for the more highly qualified students and staggering increases in tuition at both public and private institutions have resulted in students' "trading down," and most institutions have resorted to tuition discounting, some to the point of fiscal crisis. As a result of this price sensitivity, profitability is low. For the immediate future, the threat from the entry

of nontraditional competition is relatively low for the full-time undergraduate institution. Competition is considerably greater for the part-time adult captured by colleges and universities during the demographical downturn of the late 1970s and the 1980s.

2. *Graduate professional market.* Enrollments in professional graduate programs are relatively flat nationally, with the exception of executive programs. The latter, especially those with prestigious reputations, are highly profitable. However, location-bound programs are likely to receive moderate challenges from new entrants to the executive education market that offer a release from the time and place constraints of traditional executive programs.

3. *Graduate arts and sciences market.* Also experiencing relatively flat enrollments are graduate programs in the arts and sciences, which are closely tied to academic hiring. Institutional profitability is quite low for arts and sciences graduate programs, and colleges and universities rely on both external research funding and the demand for undergraduate instruction for fiscal support. The low profitability of these programs means that the threat from nontraditional providers is minimal.

Nontraditional-market students are typically part-time, employed part- or full-time, and older than twenty-five (and increasingly older than forty). They are a mixture of people seeking credentials in the form of a degree, certification, or licensure and others taking individual courses for career upgrade, career transition, or self-renewal and enrichment. In contrast to the traditional markets, programs for the nontraditional student have high growth potential and high profitability margins if costs are managed and technology costs are built into the structure from the outset. As more and more institutions seek new sources of revenues, niche programs are becoming increasingly important. This may favor the more entrepreneurial new entrants, who are more successful in identifying and targeting the needs of nontraditional and corporate students.

Mistakes Many Schools Make

Increasingly, institutions are seeking to find new markets and to develop new sources of revenue. As they move forward, however, they often fall prey to a common set of pitfalls:

- *Failure to provide adequate guidance.* Senior administrators often fail to provide guidelines for and parameters of an acceptable plan. For example, a private university seeking to increase nontraditional revenues asked its deans to develop business plans. Each of the deans was given wide latitude in how to approach the issue, and the resulting plans, not surprisingly, varied widely in their quality and specificity.

- *"If we build it, they will come."* There is no point in developing a new program unless prospective students recognize its value and are willing to pay to enroll. One private university offered a program that would allow students to take courses on a nondegree basis, provided they paid full tuition. Although twenty such students were budgeted for annually, the school never attracted more than two during the three years the program was in operation. The university had failed to recognize that students would not pay full tuition if their coursework would not count toward a degree or credential.

- *Supply-side focus.* A related problem is the lack of attention to what potential customers really want. To move quickly, institutions tend to build on existing capacity and strengths. Faculty tend to identify new programs that leverage their interests. Too little attention is paid to the basic market research that identifies market needs, targets specific clienteles, defines marketing approaches, and determines pricing strategies.

- *Program cannibalization.* Institutions often fail to ask whether the projected enrollments for new programs will reflect students who would not otherwise have enrolled at that institution or whether the program will siphon off students who would otherwise have enrolled in an existing program. New programs that increase retention are to be highly valued, but moving students around who would be there anyway provides no new net revenue.

- *Lack of specific action plans.* Having identified a new program, many plans fail to outline next steps. Defining a logical sequence of activities, milestones, and resource requirements provides the management framework necessary to translate good ideas into tangible programs.

A Public Research University That Did It Right

In the spring of 1997, the president of a leading public research university appointed a committee to determine the university's potential position in the distance education marketplace and to propose a university action plan. The committee began its assignment by preparing three working papers: a summary of the distance education context and of relevant trends and assumptions; an internal audit of the university's current offerings in distance education; and an analysis of the cable TV industry in the state, to provide an understanding of delivery options.

With this information in hand, the committee addressed the question, "How prepared is the university to pursue a distance education strategy, and where should it invest?" To answer this question, they needed to

- Assess the leadership's real commitment to distance education

- Identify readiness for distance education within the institution's units, including administrative sponsorship and commitment, faculty involvement, level of instructional activity, and infrastructure availability

- Identify cultural barriers and enablers, including policies and practices, that would affect the institution's ability to be successful

- Identify alternative strategic directions to guide institutional initiatives

- Identify program opportunities and develop business plans for three opportunities

Eager to move from planning to action, the university was most anxious to develop the business plans. However, to ensure that the plans would be developed for opportunities with the prospect of market and financial viability, it was crucial to drive toward a vision with multiple pathways. The initial analysis unveiled dozens of alternative directions, of which ten were considered viable for financial investments based on the criteria of brand recognition, institutional strengths and weaknesses, and positioning relative to competitors. Examples of the directions considered included "innovate existing curriculum content," "build from brand-name opportunities," and "provide personal enrichment opportunities."

Ultimately, guided by three preferred strategic directions, the university selected three distance education program opportunities for business plan development. The plans they developed included

- A definition of the product concept or program opportunity

- A description of current and prospective program customers

- A profile of the competition and their level of penetration in the market

- A discussion of product development issues, including product pricing, promotion, and distribution

- An examination of operational considerations, such as faculty training, technology support, instructional development, and availability of student services

- A high-level financial projection of possible costs and revenues over the initial years of program development and enhancement

- An analysis of the risks and rewards of pursuing the product venture

Armed with a concrete description of each program, knowledge of the potential and future market, the readiness of the academic unit to deliver, an understanding of the required support infrastructure, and a sense of the potential financial profits or losses, the university was positioned to make strategic investments in distance education.

Institutional Strategy: Charting a Course to Compete

Most institutions have had the same strategy for decades, with little variation in their range of program offerings or target student population. With few exceptions, the geographical boundaries that framed their strategy were the walls that defined the campus perimeter. Institutions have competed with a stable set of peer institutions with predictable patterns of competitive behavior. Under such a relatively stable set of competitive conditions, there has been little need for the rigorous business planning and competitor and market analyses frequently undertaken by corporations. Rather, colleges and universities have focused on where they can make incremental investments to raise the quality of their programs and student body through their faculty recruiting and tuition discounting strategies.

The rise of nontraditional competition significantly alters the challenges and questions that institutions now face. Today, institutions must devise strategies and tactics not only to find new sources of revenue but also to preserve the traditional sources they have enjoyed. Decision makers must consider not only their range of program offerings but also where they will compete, what programs they will compete with, how they will deliver their programs, and who is likely to compete with them.

The rapid growth of nontraditional markets for education and the expanded delivery mechanisms (for example, the Internet, distance learning, satellite campuses) create a multitude of entrepreneurial opportunities for an institution's schools, departments, and faculty. The scope and benefits of new ventures will be enormous, but so will the risks.

Deans, provosts, and presidents must view their responsibility in setting strategy as that of managing a broad portfolio of programs and opportunities in a highly dynamic market. Higher education's leadership will routinely be asked to sift through numerous proposals each year to invest in new programs. Like a venture capitalist, they must determine which programs offer the greatest potential for benefit and the greatest likelihood of success. They must have structured means for evaluating the revenue potential, investment requirements, level of quality, and level of risk associated with each new venture. As investors of scarce institutional resources, they must be able to evaluate the many opportunities laid before them, as they can fund only a relatively small group of programs. The choices that deans, provosts, and presidents make must be consistent with a broader set of institutional strategies and directions.

To evaluate and manage these new opportunities for growth effectively, institutions must put in place three critical planning components:

- Strategic guidelines and program development parameters

- A rigorous business planning process for evaluating potential new ventures

- Rapid evaluation and decision-making processes

Strategic Guidelines and Program Development Parameters

Before individual schools or faculty are asked to develop proposals for new ventures, the institution as a whole needs to define its broad strategy for competing in new markets. This will enable the institution to establish and communicate the range of new ventures they will support. For faculty, this institutional strategy provides initial criteria that they can use to self-screen their own entrepreneurial ideas for new ventures.

This institutional strategy should not be overly defined. In fact, there is a risk that a strategy that is too rigorous will be too rigid and limiting and will cause the institution to miss opportunities. Instead, the strategy should provide general definitions as to the types of new ventures that would be consistent with the institution's mission, existing strengths, and available resources.

Guidance for new program development should consider five elements:

Program Offerings

- Is the institution interested primarily in taking its traditional courses and programs of study and offering them to expanded markets? Or will the institution support the development of customized sources of study for a particular audience (for example, an MBA curriculum tailored to a single corporation)?

- Does the institution have the resources and flexibility required to rapidly alter and tailor its courses as it encounters new markets?

- Will the institution focus its programs on any one set of programs (business, for example)?

- Will it encourage some of its schools to pursue new markets (for example, professional schools) and discourage others?

Market Segments

- In which market segments will the institution compete for students?

- Do the institution's strengths lie in pursuing traditional undergraduate and graduate students?

- Does the institution have the reputation and resources to move beyond its traditional market segments?

- Can the institution reach a group of adult learners that will participate in multiple programs over the course of their lifetime?

- Will the institution market its programs directly to students? Or will it approach corporations or other organizations?

- What quality standards must be maintained as new opportunities and markets are identified?

Geographical Boundaries

- Will the institution place any restrictions on where it will compete?

- Will it view new ventures as a way to bring more students to its present campus?

- Would it consider launching satellite campuses to reach specific markets?

- Do its name recognition and existing strengths lie locally, regionally, or globally?

Delivery Methods

- Will the majority of courses be delivered through traditional classroom methods?

- To what degree will the educational delivery be virtual?

- Will the institution support the use of Internet, satellite broadcasts, or cable TV as methods of delivery for instruction?

- Are the institution's existing technical infrastructure and support services capable of supporting these types of ventures?

Investment

- What level of resources is the institution able and willing to invest in new programs?

- Are new markets being pursued as experiments to gain experience?

- Is the institution dependent on creating new revenue streams for its long-term viability?

- Is it seeking to invest heavily in a targeted set of programs that must generate large returns? Or is it considering making small investments in a broader set of programs?

Given the almost limitless potential for generating ideas for new ventures and the very real constraints of available resources, how an institution answers these questions will bring important focus to the development effort. Just as maintaining the status quo is not an acceptable option in the face of new competition, neither is doing everything.

Structured Business Planning

To optimize decisions about opportunities for new ventures, the institution must be able to consider and evaluate structured business plans. Adopting a standard approach to business planning will provide decision makers with a systematic method for evaluating and comparing individual proposals for new programs. A well-developed business plan should answer the following questions:

Market Questions

- To whom will the program be offered?

    What geographical area will it cover?

    What will be the demographical profile of a typical student?

- Why will people want to participate in the program?

    To pursue an interesting hobby?

    To fulfill a requirement for continuing professional education or certification?

    For worker retraining?

- How large is the potential market?

Program Questions

- What will the program offer?

- How will this proposal capitalize on existing institutional strengths?

    Will it utilize existing faculty?

    Will it focus on acknowledged areas of programmatic strength?

    Will it better utilize existing infrastructure?

- How will quality standards for students and curriculum be measured and maintained?

Financial Questions

- What investments will be required to develop the program? Specifically, what will be required for course development, marketing, space, and technology?

- What will its ongoing operating costs be?

- How will the program offering be priced?

    What will the tuition be?

    Will financial aid and scholarships be offered?

- What revenue will the program generate?

    In its first year?

    In subsequent years?

- What assumptions are being made in the financial model for the program being presented?

Risk Questions

- With what other institutions will this new program compete for students?

- Why will students come to this program rather than to a competitor's?

- How sensitive are the financial assumptions?

- Can the program still generate viable revenues if those assumptions are wrong by 10 percent? 25 percent? 50 percent?

- Does the program present any risk to the institution's overall reputation for quality or high academic standards?

Rapid Evaluation and Decision Making

The process of answering these questions will not only produce a business plan that can be used to explain and evaluate the new proposal, it will also refine the idea itself. The rigorous nature of the process will help further the development of the concept of a new program before it reaches any institution-wide review process. It will also cause the idea generator to perform a self-evaluation of his or her proposal and voluntarily screen out those ideas that do not appear to hold up under the scrutiny of the business planning questions.

To make the planning process effective, all plans should work through a discussion of these questions in a standard manner. Common templates for financial planning should be provided, and the format and appearance of plans should be standardized. This will provide for a more fair and efficient decision-making process. Proposals requiring larger investments should include original market research data to further validate assumptions about market demand and pricing.

Finally, institutions need to be prepared to decide quickly which programs to pursue and which to decline. In a competitive market, an opportunity identified at the beginning of a planning process might not be viable within one or two years. Traditional multiyear planning and decision making timetables will not be sustainable. Institutions must also be prepared to continuously reevaluate and adapt programs as new competitors emerge with new offerings and as the needs of students change. In approving a new venture, an institution must also identify what factors or warning signals it will look for to decide when the program should change or be shut down.

Barriers to Entry

The development of an institutional strategy for nontraditional markets must also be framed by an acknowledgment of current barriers within higher education generally and, more specifically, within each institution. Of course, not all colleges and universities share these in equal measure, and at some institutions these considerations are insignificant. But together these factors do inhibit, to one degree or another, an institution's ability to be proactive (and sometimes even its ability to be reactive). Barriers to entry include the following:

- *Fixed costs in faculty.* Faculty are often resistant to moving in new areas, and opportunities to develop new programs may result either in a commitment to new faculty lines or to the use of adjuncts that have little institutional commitment.

- *Fixed costs in the physical plant.* Colleges and universities have an incentive to fill up existing on-campus classroom space and facilities. This can inhibit their flexibility in bringing educational services out to the market.

- *Pre-Gutenberg pedagogical methodology.* As practitioners of medieval modes of teaching, the faculty (individually or collectively) are sometimes resistant to technical innovations. The recent decision by a Canadian university that professors will not be forced to use technology is a case in point.

- *Professional paradigms.* The use of sophisticated technology often demands that the instructor team with curriculum designers and technical specialists. Similarly, corporate partnerships require that curricula be developed in concert with the customer. For many professors, such collaboration constitutes an intrusion and a threat to their professional autonomy.

- *Little leverage in professorial models.* Despite its obvious virtues, face-to-face classroom interaction limits the reach of each instructor. Where institutions are unwilling or unable to leverage technology and alternative delivery methods, the economics of education will be limited by how many people can fit into the classroom.

- *Potentially large investments in technology.* Virtual education and distance learning do not come cheap. And where the corporate partnership involves technical or scientific education, there may need to be considerable investment in facilities and equipment. One university has spent over $1 million in a state-of-the-art facility for providing Novell, Microsoft, and other types of technical certification to the financial services community.

- *Nonbusiness or antibusiness orientation.* There is a strong ethos within many universities that any involvement in corporate or sponsored education is a deal with the devil. In some cases, even overt discussions of new programs as revenue generators can elicit negative reactions from the campus community.

Conclusion

This, then, is the new competitive landscape: new sets of buyers with new expectations, a growing set of competitors who see a lucrative business opportunity, and existing higher education institutions that are steeped in tradition. Ultimately, culture may be the greatest factor affecting the ability of colleges and universities to succeed in the new market.

4

The New Technologies and the Future of Residential Undergraduate Education

Gregory C. Farrington

Computers and inexpensive telecommunications have sparked a revolution in communications that is comparable to the impact of radio and television earlier in this century. The new information technologies make it possible to disseminate information faster than ever before, but their truly revolutionary aspect is that they allow each user to be a publisher of information as well as a consumer and to interact with vast numbers of people around the globe, simply, quickly, and inexpensively. With the Internet, commercial publishers are no longer the arbiters of what information is made available and by whom. It would be hard to find any industry whose vision of the future has not been changed radically by the dawn of the Internet Age.

Digital media are now challenging those most venerable information organizations—colleges and universities—to rethink the ways in which they serve society. Colleges and universities specialize in creating new knowledge, sifting and storing it, and then sharing it with the next generation. The new communications technologies offer higher education the opportunity to carry out its traditional missions with powerful new tools. Education has never been more important, and access to affordable higher education is increasingly a necessity rather than a privilege. The most imaginative colleges and universities will not hesitate to use the new technologies to make education more effective, more affordable, and more accessible as well.

Some of the most promising new applications of information technology are in programs of postgraduate education designed to provide lifelong learning for mature students. Digital media have liberated traditional educational institutions from the constraints of their real estate and now allow them to deliver courses and programs to new and often untraditional groups of students wherever they may be in the world. Many of the more innovative institutions are already exploring these new educational opportunities or, to use a very unacademic word that is destined to be heard more and more, their new markets.

What, then, in this new world of high-speed communication lines, compressed video, laptops, and distance education, is the future of the undergraduate experience, particularly residential undergraduate education? What of the freshman year, all-night study sessions, cramming for finals, and calls home for money? What of the football team? Will the world of undergraduate education that most of us recall so fondly disappear, transformed into a virtual experience on a glowing screen?

One certainly hopes not, but surely the new technologies can be used to make residential undergraduate education more effective. Doing so will take a great deal of experimentation, the goal of which should be to improve what can be made better, leave alone what is working just fine, and have the good sense to know the difference. This chapter explores some of the opportunities digital technologies offer for improving residential undergraduate education and suggests, as well, aspects that would be better left alone.

Who Goes to College, and Why?

The image of ivy-covered walls, faculty in tweeds, and students debating literature and science in institutions cushioned by large endowments, for all of its romantic resonance, is a reality for only a small fraction of the undergraduate student population in America. In fact, the United States today has about 3,600 institutions of higher education, which accommodate more than fourteen million students. Approximately two-thirds of each year's high school graduates in the United States pursue some form of college education. Roughly half of them attend community colleges, institutions that often are non-residential, serve students of a wide range of ages, and have a strong focus on equipping graduates for employment. Only about one-sixth of America's college students study in residential institutions, and only a small number of these colleges and universities have substantial endowments. Most principally derive their income, whether from their state legislature or from parents, from teaching.

Most students pursue higher education to get a good job. Relatively few, unfortunately, have the freedom to study simply for the sheer joy of learning. Whether the goal is a one-year certificate for an entry-level computer position or a full four-year degree possibly leading to further advanced education, students justify the cost of higher education for its power to ensure their economic future. This reality is reflected in the distribution of academic majors. According to U.S. Department of Education statistics for 1991, of the one million bachelor's degrees awarded that year, 7,300 were in philosophy and religion, 12,000 were in foreign languages, and about 250,000 were in business.

In considering the future of undergraduate educational institutions in the Internet Age, it is important to keep in mind that these institutions already take many different forms and serve many different kinds of students. The ivied campus, although wonderful, is only one of many worlds of higher education—and one of the smallest, as well.

Laptops in Ten Years

What, then, is the technological future? The rate at which digital technologies are developing is so fast that most of us cannot keep up, let alone adapt. Looking backward helps a little to imagine the future. Little more than a decade ago, computers were midgets compared with today's PCs, screens were black and white, "portable" computers had very strong handles, e-mail was something of a curiosity, and the Internet was used by only a few. The revolutionary technology of the time was the fax machine, along with answering machines and word processors.

Now, only ten years later, audio and video clips are dispatched around the world at the touch of the "send" button, life without e-mail seems inconceivable, the Internet is the start for many trips of exploration, and homes will soon have high-speed data links that merge entertainment, information, communication, and computing.

Looking a decade into the future is difficult even for someone in the eye of the digital whirlwind, but some good guesses can be made as to how it will develop. Laptop computers will become far more powerful, compact, and cheaper at the same time. It will be easier and easier to carry computers with us all the time, wherever we go. Desktop computers also will become even more powerful and less expensive, with new integrated circuits, new memory technology, and flat-panel screens. Homes will be connected to the Internet and new media providers by high-speed data networks. In terms of communications and computing power, a good assumption is that within ten years inexpensive technology will allow each of us to send and receive video, audio, graphics, and text, synchronously or asynchronously, wherever we are in the world. The personal computer–television screen will be a video window on the world. Computers will also develop more and more powerful capabilities for interacting with humans like humans, through powerful simulation, visualization, and speech recognition. In fact, many of these changes will already be upon us in five years, not ten.

Learning Is Not Entertainment, and Education Is Not Baseball

In this dizzying rush into the future, it is important to keep in mind that the challenge for education in ten or twenty years will be the same as it is today: to educate real people, not computers, and to stimulate them to learn, not to entertain them. It is easy to be dizzied by techno-enthusiasm and imagine that computers will change people and how human minds learn. However, for a long time to come, learning will remain hard work, requiring not only information but also interaction, practice, and discipline. Yes, it is fun to frolic with the new media tools, but it is important to keep in mind that human heads are not filled with computer chips (not yet, at least). Learning is not the same as downloading.

One often hears that the new tools of communication will make it possible for one master professor, presumably one sitting under a palm tree on a warm island in the Caribbean, to educate thousands of students at a time. The implication is that hundreds of faculty with lesser minds will be put out of work and replaced by a small international cadre of superstars. This vision is analogous to many of the changes that did, in fact, occur in sports when radio and then television made it possible for fans everywhere to follow only a few professional sports teams instead of cheering the hundreds and thousands of local teams whose playing was not quite so good. As a result, interest in local teams faded and was replaced by national professional sports mania. Recordings and radio had much the same effect on local orchestras.

But education is not baseball. Learning requires engagement and interaction. If one master teacher could replace dozens of local hitters, then videotapes would have put hundreds of faculty out of business long ago. Videotapes didn't because they do not provide any way for students to interact with one another and with the teacher. The big star on the tape does not hold office hours, grade homework assignments, give exams, and provide the discipline that forces students to convert information into learning. Armchair baseball fans do not need to learn to hit, but students do. Learning is not a spectator sport.

Nevertheless, the new media do present provocative opportunities for improving education and possibly making it less expensive.

To explore them, it is important to keep in mind that the way we teach today is neither the only nor the best way. New is not necessarily better, but neither is old. The current model of teaching at the college level is widely taken as the "right way" not because it is, but because it has worked for a long time and the forces for change have not been too great. Lectures and discussion, combined with practice in the form of homework, laboratory experiments, and similar exercises, all integrated by the discipline of a regular schedule, grading, and examinations, have been and still are a very effective method of educating large numbers of students at a reasonable cost.

Traditionally, teaching has been largely a cottage industry. Each faculty member has selected the information he or she plans to teach, produced it in the form needed for instruction (notes, overhead transparencies, homework problems), delivered it in person, devised all sorts of methods for encouraging students to engage and learn, and then assessed each student's performance. The process has involved far more than just the delivery of information, which is a relatively simple task and could well be replaced by a video clip. The expensive part has been the interaction, engagement, and assessment; one might say that what students pay for is not so much the batting theory but the practice time at bat.

With the new digital technologies, students no longer need to sit in a classroom all together at the same time to access a professor's lecture. Similarly, the powerful visualization capabilities of computers can be used to present information in ways that are often more effective than print. Increasingly powerful software enables computers to interact with students more and more as humans do, to help them learn skills in subjects as diverse as foreign languages, mathematics, and music. Most importantly, the digital technologies connect students and faculty so that they can discuss and debate with one another without being present in the same place at the same time.

Certainly, student-teacher interaction via e-mail is different from in-person interaction. On the one hand, those who have experienced Web-based teaching will attest that in many instances e-mail interaction is more personal and intimate than live interaction. It gives the student and teacher more time for thoughtful reflection and can help lower the natural barriers that exist between expert and novice. On the other hand, e-mail interaction is slow; it is hard to imagine a Web-based discussion breaking into the lively and infectious debate possible in a live setting. Of course, for most students and faculty e-mail and Web interaction are simply one additional method of communicating and certainly not the only means by which they interact. Web-based discussion will most likely only increase the participants' interest in meeting and talking "for real."

In fact, it will take quite some time and a great deal more research before the best uses of the new technologies in education are sorted out. What is clear, however, is that change will happen—and at a rate not seen in education for a long time. In most colleges and universities, *innovation* has traditionally been a term associated with research and scholarship, not teaching methods. The new digital technologies now make bold and creative educational experimentation possible, and some colleges and universities will take advantage of the opportunities to innovate and become more attractive for students as a result.

Will the University of Phoenix Replace the Ivy League?

It is hard to find a college or university that does not have some faculty, generally the zealous pioneers, who are experimenting with the use of computers and the Internet in teaching. For the most part, their experiments are evolutionary in that they are using the new tools to teach the way they have always taught, just more efficiently and effectively. What they are doing is important but so far poses little threat to the football team.

However, truly bold and revolutionary experiments using telecommunications to create programs of distance education also are under way. The University of Phoenix is one of the most provoca-tive. A private, for-profit corporation organized to serve working adults, the University of Phoenix takes a very student-oriented approach (they surely call it a customer-oriented approach). Phoenix holds classes in the evening, at times and locations convenient for working students. Faculty primarily are practitioners who actually work during the day in the fields that they teach at night. Tenure does not exist, and faculty who do not teach well presumably do not teach for long. Today, most University of Phoenix classes are "real" in that they are based on real-time, synchronous classroom education at distrib-uted sites in locations across the United States. However, it is clear that the University of Phoenix is shifting quickly to develop asyn-chronous distance education programs delivered via the Internet.

Many faculty and administrators at traditional colleges may be tempted to dismiss the University of Phoenix as being just one step from a mail-order degree mill and therefore not to be taken seri-ously, but doing so is risky. Certainly, a major challenge for organi-zations like the University of Phoenix is that of achieving a high quality of education for their students. The University of Phoenix states that it carries out a rigorous program of quality assessment, and it certainly is in their interest to do so. Some critics may assert that the interaction that occurs between teacher and student in a University of Phoenix–type context may in fact produce training, but surely not education. In fact, the process by which study leads to true education and not simply the learning of skills is elusive in any setting and very much influenced by the motivations of the stu-dent and teacher and the style of the program of learning. Assuming that a different medium of interaction necessarily dooms the qual-ity of learning to that of skill acquisition would seem to be a some-what hasty response of the traditionalist to the new. Regardless, a key challenge for distance education, just as for traditional residen-tial education, is to stimulate students to go beyond facts and skills and create in themselves the deeper intellectual structures that define, however imprecisely, the goal of a true education.

Despite these concerns, the University of Phoenix is proving to be quite popular. It claims to have more than forty thousand students enrolled, many of whom are earning accredited bachelor's degrees in fields such as business, nursing, and education, as well as MBA degrees. The credit-hour cost brings the total for an undergraduate degree to approximately $20,000, much lower than most residential institutions. In addition, University of Phoenix students can earn while they learn: they do not spend four years away from real jobs while preparing to find one.

The University of Phoenix model is quite challenging, even threatening, to traditional institutions. The goal of the University of Phoenix is to deliver good-quality education to students who need it and are willing to pay for it, wherever they live or work and at a price they can afford. The University of Phoenix will ultimately succeed or fail based on its ability to do just that.

Granted, few would suggest that an MBA from the University of Phoenix will open the door to the executive suite as quickly as one from Wharton or Harvard will, and few would imagine that the most capable and talented students will soon choose the University of Phoenix over more traditional programs. However, the University of Phoenix is still young, and the competition has just begun. Clearly, the University of Phoenix is going for the market in which it can succeed at this stage of its development. Competing with high-end programs aimed at the country's top students would be a bad business strategy, at least at the start; but what of the future? Might a University of Phoenix find a way to deliver a program of undergraduate education in, for example, business, mathematics, or engineering that is comparable to those available at the finest traditional universities?

If the University of Phoenix or an organization like it were to decide to compete for the top students, its first step would be to choose a degree with a high value. Then it would assemble the finest faculty, establish high standards for admissions, produce an exceptionally fine program, and deliver it to students wherever they live and work and charge them a fair price for it. It would be critical to ensure that the faculty, the students, and the educational program itself were truly outstanding by conventional measures. If these steps were followed and the program prospered, it would soon establish its own reputation for excellence. In fact, at least one major corporation has already begun exploring how to create an MBA program of this sort.

Among more traditional institutions, the Fuqua School of Business at Duke University appears to have taken these steps in designing their new Global Executive MBA program that is delivered via a combination of on-site and distance education techniques. Though some traditionalists may sniff that it is not the equivalent of a residential program, its success will ultimately be determined by the marketplace. If it is intellectually excellent, attracts outstanding students, and is perceived to be a good value for the price, then it is likely to succeed and, in doing so, challenge traditional programs that require students to live away from their homes and jobs for twelve to twenty-four months. Its success will be the direct result of harnessing the power of the new digital media technologies to deliver education and facilitate interaction among students and faculty who are widely separated in distance.

A half dozen or more initiatives like the University of Phoenix have already been started. One is the Western Governors University, in which several states in the western United States are cooperating in using the new digital technologies to bring undergraduate education to off-campus students throughout the region and beyond, again through the power of telecommunications. Others include University-On-Line (UOL), Caliber Learning Systems, and Real Education. These are all for-profit corporations whose goal is to make money by delivering high-quality education to students who need it and are motivated to pursue and pay for it. In each of these cases, the main impact of the new digital and telecommunications technologies is to make educational experimentation and innovation possible and therefore to make competition with traditional institutions inevitable.

One reason these new programs are promising is that their style tends to attract students who are highly motivated to learn. Presumably most of their students have full-time jobs, are paying for their own education, and thus are keenly aware of its cost both in terms of money and time. These students provide their own discipline to do the hard work that learning requires.

Can this approach work with the average eighteen-year-old undergraduate? So much depends on discipline and motivation. The years between the ages of about eighteen and twenty-five are a time in which young men and women sort out their options. Some do it in the Marines, many more do it in community colleges, and a few do it in the Ivy League; but whichever way they spend the time, it is the capstone of an extended adolescence. Not many first-year college students—even the smartest and most capable ones—are mature enough to succeed outside of a structured learning environment (particularly those from more affluent backgrounds). A large part of what traditional colleges and universities provide is the structure and discipline young college students need to thrive. So the University of Phoenix and similar organizations are unlikely to put the Ivy League out of business anytime soon. Most traditional undergraduates are simply not sufficiently self-directed to manage this kind of educational program.

However, the University of Phoenix may prove to be a very attractive alternative for students who would otherwise enroll in a local community college part-time while working to support themselves. Another important role for the University of Phoenix is in providing a second chance at a degree for students who have taken a bit more time to recognize the importance of earning one. Traditional four-year colleges and universities design their undergraduate programs almost exclusively for fresh high school graduates, not for returning adult students. Again, older students are largely served today by community colleges. One suspects that University-On-Line, the Western Governors University, and similar distance education undergraduate programs also will tend to attract students who are somewhat older than is traditional, students who have come to understand that education matters a great deal to their future and thus are highly motivated to study.

It seems likely, therefore, that the University of Phoenix and other programs like it will provide the stiffest competition to many of the community colleges and smaller private colleges that survive on tuition income from students of many ages. Some of these institutions, particularly those that are private, are financially fragile. One would hope that they recognize the growing competition and are working very hard to compete in such a way that their residential programs offer far more than can ever be delivered over a telecommunications line.

New Media and Traditional Education

Fortunately, many fresh high school graduates will still choose to invest in a traditional residential undergraduate experience and will be able to find the means to do so. For them, undergraduate life at a residential college is as much about learning to live as it is about learning from books. What is most impressive about the residential college experience is that it works so well and achieves both goals so effectively. Eighteen-year-old students nervously tiptoe onto campus at the start of their first year, and four years later they march out—sometimes after a bit of prodding, to be sure, but generally with the motivation, education, and confidence needed to take on the world. The transformation is remarkable and is as much the product of the general intellectual and social experience on campus as the result of what goes on formally in the classroom. For these students, late-night discussions are much of what college is about, and the role of the football team is truly important. It is hard to imagine distance education, however effective, being an equivalent.

What, then, might be the reasons to use the new digital media in traditional residential undergraduate programs? There really are two: one is to make residential education better, and the other is to reduce its cost. Imagining ways to use the new media to make residential education better is easy; making it less expensive will be more challenging.

Experiments in the use of the new technologies in undergraduate education are going on in most institutions of higher education. A good example is the use of campus networks to broadcast course information, class notes, and homework assignments. Another is the growing use of chat groups to supplement in-class discussion. Still other uses exploit the powerful ability of multimedia to enhance learning.

At the University of Pennsylvania, where I was previously dean of the School of Engineering and Applied Science, such uses of multimedia and telecommunications are already common. In some departments it is hard to find a course that does not have a Web page, and increasingly the Net is being used as a medium for class discussion. For example, intense conversations about language and meaning go on at all hours in a listserv run by Professor Al Filreis of the English Department to support his class in poetry. He has found that students often will talk to a screen more candidly than to one another in class, particularly those students who missed class. On a keyboard, the thoughtful have time to think and the shy have courage to speak, and the tedious can be deleted by the merciful stroke of a key or two.

The Web has liberated many faculty in Penn's History of Art Department from old-fashioned slide projectors. Their students can now access the rich collection of visual materials needed to study art by using the campus network, which makes a big difference the night before an exam.

Many other applications of the new media to make education better can be conceived. Few of them are likely to make it significantly more efficient or less expensive. If anything, they increase the cost of running a campus, what with the demand for fast networks, wired dormitories, computers that regularly need fixing and upgrading, and a staff of highly paid professionals to keep all the technological systems humming.

Another characteristic of these first-generation experiments is that they are mostly variations on the traditional model of teaching, which assumes that faculty deliver information to students through the medium of the lecture and that students and faculty interact mostly in the formal classroom.

Of course, the traditional combination of lecture, recitation, and homework can be extraordinarily effective and efficient. Some universities—very fine universities, in fact—have lecture classes of five hundred to eight hundred students, each featuring a true faculty star. The lectures are then augmented by extensive recitation sessions handled by graduate students. The large lecture may not be a very personal experience, but it certainly can be powerful in the hands of a real master of both substance and technique. Certainly, from an educational standpoint, it would be more interesting to have the same lecturer stand in front of only fifty students and actually engage them in conversation and debate. However, an institution that chooses to offer a course with one star and five hundred to eight hundred students is making a decision that is both economic and intellectual. What is lost in terms of the personal touch is, one hopes, gained by exposing a larger number of students to the exceptional professor. The total educational impact, as we all know, can be every effective, if the star is really a star, the recitation leaders know their stuff, and the students are smart. It is hard indeed to imagine doing better with multimedia.

However, not all faculty are stars, not all recitation leaders know their stuff, and not all students thrive in such big classes. In addition, relatively few subjects can attract five hundred to eight hundred students at one time. At many private institutions, classes tend to be relatively small, each enrolling between ten and forty students. In addition, the idea that "one size fits all"—that is, that one method of instruction, the lecture-recitation model, is best for all subjects—seems intuitively illogical. Yet few, if any, classes are ever designed by first posing the question of how students might best learn. It somehow is assumed that, whatever the topic, a professor should stand in front of a class and deliver information, students should feverishly take inaccurate and incomplete notes, and teaching should be done as it always has been done.

Some subjects invite far more radical experiments in learning using the new media. Beginning science and math are good examples. It takes an optimistic professor indeed to believe that first-year students learn much physics by sitting through a set of introductory physics lectures. In fact, most students actually learn beginning physics (and more advanced versions as well) when they sit down and grapple with the course content, either in the form of a text or notes, and the problems that accompany it. The lecture may actually be mostly a waste of everyone's time, but it is a ritual that is followed out of habit (on the part of faculty) or out of fear of missing something that might be on the exam (on the part of students).

Possibly a better approach might be to convert the entire course content in introductory physics into a Web-based format, in a Web site that includes text, illustrations, and even an audio lecture broken into five- to ten-minute segments. Students could then access the core information on their own schedule, repeating sections as much as they choose, and then devote classroom time to discussions of recent research results, problem sets, questions, and all the topics that only humans can address. In other words, use the Web to do what it can do well, which is to present information in a variety of formats twenty-four hours a day, and save live class time for the intellectual interactions that only humans can provide.

Professor Keith Ross of Penn's School of Engineering has already created a very interesting course designed around these principles. He produced a complete one-semester course that uses Internet-based instruction, appropriately on the topic of telecommunications and designed for upper-level undergraduates and master's students. His goal was to eliminate the classroom as the focus of teaching and to make it possible for a heterogeneous group of students, including some who live on campus and others who are employed full-time, to participate on their own schedules, while maintaining a lively intellectual interaction between the students and the professor.

Professor Ross began by recording his regular class lectures, editing them, and then rerecording them in more polished form. Each lecture was then divided into audio segments, each approximately ten minutes long, and then supplemented by appropriate simulations and illustrations. Each student accessed all of this material over the World Wide Web and could listen to the lecture clips and review the material as many times as he or she wished. The Web site also served as a medium for discussion. The professor and students posted discussion topics and questions, and all participants joined in an asynchronous discussion of the class material. Papers and homework exercises were also dealt with over the Web.

This class was offered for the first time in complete form during the regular fall semester of 1997, and more than forty students chose it over a conventional live version presented at the same time. The class met once at the start of the semester and then twice more for formal examinations. At the end, most students were quite enthusiastic about the experience, in particular about the freedom they had had to study on their own schedules and to interact closely with the professor, albeit online. In addition, there was no indication from student performance that the online students were at any intellectual disadvantage because of their nontraditional experience. The course is unquestionably a provocative model for making education in appropriate subjects more effective.

What this approach did not do was to save the professor, the university, or the students any time or money. Professor Ross estimated that he spent about 50 percent more time than usual in teaching, mostly in direct interactions with the students through Web-based discussion. In fact, the course was more interactive and more personal than it would have been had it been presented traditionally, a point that is actually not so surprising, even if some find it counterintuitive. It would be virtually impossible for one professor to deal with more than forty or fifty students in this way, simply because of the intensity of the discussions that go on. However, larger classes could be accommodated through the use of online teaching fellows or through more careful organization of the online discussion.

From a pedagogical standpoint, there are many advantages to this type of Web-based teaching. One is that a course can be improved steadily, screen by screen and lecture by lecture, and thus grow in effectiveness and quality each year in a way that simply does not happen in the traditional format. In addition, guest lecturers can be easily incorporated, so that a truly superb version of a course can be built up over several cycles and then still be available for students even if the originating professor goes on sabbatical or needs a break. Another key advantage is the high intensity of the student-student and student-professor interaction. This approach also lends itself quite nicely to the sharing of a faculty member from one institution among several others—certainly more easily than does the more sophisticated technology of live distance video production.

Perhaps the most successful use of this teaching style could be in a hybrid form, in which the Web is used to deliver fundamental information that would otherwise be the subject of a lecture and as a medium for extended discussion. Class time would not be eliminated but would be replaced by more informal meetings of a seminar type and devoted to more free-ranging discussion. As mentioned earlier, this model might be particularly appropriate for teaching introductory math and science courses to large numbers of students who may have quite different backgrounds. It would allow those with more experience to move ahead quickly and those who need more time to take it.

Another reason for exploring the use of the Web as a medium of instruction is the rapid growth of simulation software for education. Software for teaching foreign languages is just one example. These programs are already so sophisticated that it is hard to imagine learning a new language without one. They virtually compel the redesign of traditional foreign language instruction. This ability of the computer to interact with a user as if the computer were a real person makes it possible to develop increasingly powerful learning programs for many other subjects as well, including science, math, and medicine. It is inevitable that such programs will become more and more sophisticated; the market is so large that the investment required to create them is justified. It remains for educators to determine how to use them in traditional programs of instruction.

The fact is that educators already have at their disposal a great variety of new software tools for teaching, and the number will only grow. Using them effectively requires fresh thinking. Truly improving education with the new media will require faculty to start with a blank page, to explore how best to teach each course, and to listen closely to students as they comment on whether it really works.

Taking advantage of the new media to improve education in this fundamental way is not a casual business. Exploiting the power of the World Wide Web in teaching is not necessarily simple or inexpensive. Faculty will need substantial help in terms of staff support and equipment. Most importantly, faculty will have to pay far more attention to innovation in teaching than has been common in the past, and administrations will have to reward them for it.

The overall goal should be to make residential undergraduate education more effective by using computers to do what they do best and freeing faculty to devote more time to students on an individual basis. The goal should be a more personal educational experience, not a dehumanized system of learning by machine. Ultimately it is human interaction, discussion, debate, experimentation, and inspiration that are truly worth four years of time and tuition. If multimedia can be used to make undergraduate education more personally interactive and more effective, then faculty should lead the way in redesigning undergraduate programs to achieve these goals.

Can Multimedia Make Residential Undergraduate Education Less Expensive?

Some people have proposed that the use of multimedia can significantly reduce the cost of residential undergraduate education.

However, much of the cost of residential undergraduate education is for services that computers cannot replace, and much of the value of a residential college is in its existence as a human community. With or without computers, students still have to eat and sleep, and it is hard to imagine how computers will make the dormitories or the food service much less expensive to operate. Computers are not likely to make people any smaller or less hungry.

The most expensive resource in teaching is faculty and staff time. The economics of instruction reduce to two factors: the amount of time a faculty member spends teaching and the number of students he or she teaches during that time. Unless the new technologies can be used to increase the average teaching productivity of faculty, there is virtually no chance that those technologies will improve the economics of traditional higher education.

There are two principal ways to increase teaching productivity using digital media. One is to use technology to share faculty among different institutions and thus eliminate redundancy in teaching capacity. The other is to exploit the powerful interactivity and simulation capabilities of computers so that digital media can be substituted for humans in the teaching process.

Video technology is already being used to share faculty among campuses. One particularly fine example is Oklahoma State University, in Stillwater, Oklahoma, which has very sophisticated video production and network facilities with which education can be delivered across the state and beyond. Many other state systems have them as well, but what about private institutions? Will it be long before Swarthmore College, Haverford College, the University of Pennsylvania, and Princeton University share content and teaching over a local video network? It is hard to say. So much depends on how quickly the technology can become truly user-friendly and robust. The more that teaching via video link requires professional-quality television production, the less it will be used by small institutions, particularly private institutions that are not part of larger systems. All indications are that studio-type distance video technology will become less expensive and easier to use. However, it is unlikely that it will become so simple that it can be operated without dedicated staff. Thus it will be economical only on a large scale, a factor that may reduce its effectiveness for small institutions.

In contrast, personal video technology is developing quickly and soon should be useful for regular faculty and students. Powerful software tools will make it possible for a class of students and their professor to interact over the network through audio, text, video, simulation, and discussion. Each faculty office and dorm room will have the capacity to become a television studio by means of a golf-ball-sized camera small enough to sit on top of a PC screen. With this deceptively simple equipment, the image of a professor or a student can be sent around the world. As networks become more and more powerful, which is happening rapidly, these tools of distance discussion and collaboration will become even easier to use and more effective.

Again, virtually any method one can conceive of to reduce the cost of residential undergraduate education achieves its goal by increasing the number of students taught by each faculty member. Distance learning technology that allows faculty to be shared among institutions is the most obvious way of doing so. A major advantage of this teaching approach will be in reducing redundancy in teaching resources. Institutions will, at least in theory, be able to eliminate small and underenrolled departments without losing access to those subject areas for their students. The teaching of relatively obscure foreign languages comes quickly to mind.

Other experiments that may reduce costs can also be imagined, in particular ones that substitute learning from a computer for being educated by a real person in the classroom. Many of these educational approaches may in fact be quite effective, but they must be explored carefully to ensure that educational quality is maintained and, preferably, improved.

Of course, most university administrators today do not associate e-mail, computers, and telecommunications with lower costs. Most are keenly aware of the high cost of installing and maintaining the new arteries of communication, not to mention the hundreds or thousands of computers needed on campus to provide access to the network. Realistically, however, it is hard to imagine that any college or university will choose to cloister itself and, like some secular order of monks, choose to operate without computers and the Internet. Computers and fast communications have simply become essential for scholarly communication—and for academic management as well. Most undergraduate students would find it bizarre to imagine enrolling in an institution that had chosen to isolate itself from the world and the World Wide Web. The challenge, therefore, is to use the new tools in such a way that the institution's investment in them provides maximum return.

Innovative Institutions Must Change

Arguably the most important consequence of the new digital media for higher education is that they make major innovations in education possible. In the past, traditional educational methods and institutions have had a monopoly on higher education. Even if the capstone intellectual and social experience provided by residential undergraduate education is indeed one of the finest preparations a student can receive for the rest of his or her life, it is clear that current models of that experience are expensive. High cost invites innovation and competition, and the new media provide tools that make both possible.

Of course, traditional faculty are generally very creative individuals. Campuses bubble with innovation, but its focus is more on scholarship than on pedagogy. Outstanding faculty scholarship is essential for high-quality education, but so is faculty and administration commitment to innovation and excellence in teaching. Too often, faculty are paid for teaching but rewarded for scholarship. Their creative energy is therefore primarily focused on the latter. This asymmetry in creativity, in which the activities that pay the bills receive the least creative energy, should be brought into greater balance.

The new media invite a thoughtful rethinking of how students are taught, not simply a nudging and tweaking of the established curricula. The marketplace will help make this happen. Traditional institutions, driven to demonstrate that their educational programs are better than the competition's and enticed by the use of digital media to do so, are likely to invest more resources in pedagogical innovation than they have in the past.

Through all of these changes, residential undergraduate campuses will be challenged to truly be what they generally claim to be—rich and lively intellectual communities in which students and faculty collaborate to discover, understand, and apply new knowledge. Scholarly and learning communities of this sort thrive on live, personal interaction. A network of high-speed telecommunications lines can never replace that interaction. Colleges and universities that understand that outstanding personal education is arguably their principal mission in society have little to fear from the Internet Age.

Will some institutions be at risk? Yes, particularly those that fail to understand that students will increasingly have alternatives and that the comfortable and rather monopolistic world that educational institutions have enjoyed for so long is shifting and changing. The market for education is large and growing. For-profit corporations will enter it aggressively and give traditional institutions real competition. Heightened competition will force educational institutions to be much more aware of the niche each fills or chooses to fill in the educational marketplace. Strategic decisions that may have been made by default in the past will have to be made far more deliberately. It is likely that colleges and universities will become more differentiated and have more distinct strategic missions in terms of the type of students they work to attract, the programs they offer, and the role of research and scholarship in their academic life.

Although the directions that change will take are not so certain, it is clear that the coming several decades will be times of major innovation in education at all levels. Traditional institutions can be leaders or spectators. The smart ones will choose to be the former.

5

Developing and Using Technology as a Strategic Asset

William H. Graves

Most colleges and universities are scrambling today to increase their return on investment in information technology (IT). But until recent years, most treated IT as a cost to be minimized rather than as an institutional investment to be judiciously increased to balance budgetary realities with future aspirations. Indeed, IT is no longer an experimental tool to be made available with minimal support to a few employees and students. Instead, it is a strategic asset that should be utilized by the entire faculty, staff, and student body to increase the productivity of mission-critical academic programs and the administrative services that support those programs. And nothing is more mission-critical in higher education than instruction!

The Internet and its World Wide Web, still largely untamed as a new instructional frontier, have become today's primary levers for increasing the effectiveness of colleges and universities and extending their reach. The Internet revolution also accounts for the fundamental paradox that animates any discussion of how best to invest in IT as a strategic asset. Battin (1989, p. 369) has eloquently articulated that paradox: "[IT] makes possible an unprecedented decentralization of technical power to individual option while at the same time it requires a globally coordinated infrastructure to permit the effective individual exercise of that power."

Battin's paradox starts at the institutional level and binds together three sets of critical issues addressed in this chapter:

1. What should be the nature and scope of the services provided by a central IT organization, and how should that organization be organized to optimize its effectiveness?

2. What institutional processes, organizational and governance structures, and economic models are most likely to lead to an integrated set of network-delivered mission-critical applications that keep pace with changes in technology?

3. What support models for instructional technology, in particular, are most likely to help the faculty and the administration use online communications tools and online learning resources to achieve the goals of the instructional mission?

These issues must be addressed in parallel. Such is the nature of Battin's paradox—everything is connected to everything else on the network. This powerful, boundary-blurring interconnectedness accounts for the Internet revolution in global communications and resource sharing and makes the issues raised here inseparable and critical to any institution. There is no one-size-fits-all set of solutions to these issues. There are, however, some general principles and a model for managing and funding the evolution of IT services that can be utilized in almost any institution as a framework for increasing the return on investment (ROI) in IT in the context of Battin's paradox. The implications of this general framework for the instructional program are noted throughout this chapter and are then specifically addressed in the closing section.

Principles for Optimizing Investments in IT

This section offers six general principles for funding and managing IT resources with the goal of maximizing ROI.

1. *An institution's total IT investment should serve institutional strategic interests but be administered with enough flexibility to encourage and support innovation and entrepreneurship in the institution's departments.* What is optimal for the institution may not be optimal

for a department or an individual. Conversely, what is optimal for a department or individual may not be optimal for the institution. Whether IT is centrally or locally funded and managed, IT support should be as accommodating and accessible to the individual as possible; yet, central support should be prioritized and funded to serve strategic institutional goals.

In higher education, nothing is more strategic than the instructional program, which also accounts for the heft of an institution's education and general expenses. Accordingly, instructional technology is becoming a critical issue as colleges and universities attempt to optimize their ROI in IT. With a mandate to increase institutional ROI, many institutions would do well to focus their investments in instructional technology on the ten to twenty introductory courses that typically account for 40 to 50 percent of their enrollments. Twigg (1995) noted the institutional payoff that could result from focusing on these courses.

Another approach is to focus on professional programs in which competitive forces are driving the need to change instructional delivery models to take advantage of new technologies. In any case, institutions should be aware that open grant programs designed to attract widespread individual faculty interest in instructional technology often result in episodic, ad hoc solutions that neither serve broader institutional interests nor scale to a sustainable level over time. The instructional technology support needs of pioneering instructors with a bent toward early-adopter experimentation are fundamentally different from the support needs of the faculty at large. Most instructors have little interest in suffering the pain associated with the bleeding edge of alpha or beta IT instructional services.

2. *Formal institutional processes are required for selecting, developing or customizing, and installing any mission-critical application. These formal processes should include input from both the central IT organization and a representative group of stakeholders, but a senior IT officer should hold veto power in the final selection decision.* In some cases, such as institutional e-mail, where there is no single application "owner,"

the central IT organization should seize the responsibility for selecting and managing the application—whether centrally or as a distributed system. In other cases, such as an institutional financial system or a set of Web-based tools to support instruction, the central IT organization should not necessarily have responsibility for selecting the application but should have a voice in the decision, along with representative clients of the system. However, even when the senior technology officer does not manage the department that has primary responsibility for the decision-making process, that officer should have veto power over the final decision, to ensure compliance with the institutional IT architecture (standards) and support capability—because everything is connected to everything else on the network that the central IT organization must support, including a baseline of networked applications.

Instructional technology support presents special challenges. Even the most technically astute instructors are not likely to judge new instructional technology opportunities by their implications for institutional affordability, scalability, and supportability. Moreover, a senior technology officer is more likely than most instructors to be aware of the latest technologies with instructional promise but is less likely to be a good judge of the practical reality of that promise from an instructional or departmental perspective. These possible disconnects argue for a process that involves the central IT leadership, academic departments, and key faculty leaders in shaping an institutional approach to supporting the use of online resources and communications tools in instruction.

3. *An institution's senior IT officer should be involved in any institution-wide strategic planning and budgeting processes. In turn, the central IT organization should assume responsibility for communicating the institution's strategic vision for the deployment and use of IT and for reporting progress toward achieving that goal.* Any institutional strategic planning process today will immediately raise a host of IT-related opportunities and issues. That is certainly true of curriculum planning and of planning for faculty development programs. Thus, on the one

hand, the presence of IT leadership at the institutional planning and budgeting table will help ensure that the institution develops the understanding required to invest wisely in IT for strategic purposes. On the other hand, any planning and budgeting process that focuses solely on IT can lead to unwise expenditures if it is not informed by the institution's strategic priorities. Placing IT leadership at the institutional planning table creates a crossroads where institutional priorities can intersect IT planning and spending to the benefit of the institution. Communication, cross-fertilization, and institutional purposes can prosper in such an environment. This is one of the critical expectations associated with cabinet-level positions popularly referred to today as chief information officer (CIO) positions (discussed in more detail later in the chapter).

In the case of instruction, there are likely to be as many instructional technology "solutions" as there are academic departments in the absence of institutional coordination. A CIO can help identify common technical requirements and create a common IT framework for new instructional support services that are institutionally scalable and supportable.

4. *Funding for an institution's central IT support organization should be placed on a recurring life cycle basis to the extent possible and should not overly rely on one-time sources or depreciation schedules not attuned to the rapid pace of technological change.* Most of today's hardware configurations have at most a three-year life expectancy, and software is typically upgraded every twelve to eighteen months. Reliance on one-time funding or unrealistic depreciation schedules seriously limits the ability to accommodate these life cycles and meet other contingencies that accompany technological change. One-time institutional funding sources are typically very competitive, and an allocation to the central IT organization can introduce additional tension into what is too often already a strained relationship between central and departmental IT support advocates competing for scarce resources. McClure, Smith, and Sitko (1997) have described this tension as being of crisis

proportions, in a monograph that should be required reading among senior administrators.

Instructional technology again poses a special challenge. Too many institutions undertake special instructional technology initiatives—grants to the faculty, for example—without accounting for the recurring life cycle resource implications of the success of such initiatives. Unlike administrative application systems and the personnel that support them, instructional technologies and attendant support personnel have only recently, if at all, been identified as a central budget responsibility and have generally not been included as a mission-critical component in budget planning exercises.

5. *All of an institution's students and employees should have convenient and affordable access to a personal computer, with a basic collection of productivity software, that can be connected to the institution's network at any time and from almost any place they are working—the office, a library, a home or residence hall, a field location, or another remote location.* Just as universal access to a telephone handset and a telephone connection enables the greatest ROI in an institution's telephone network, universal access to a PC and a connection to the Internet is a core requirement for increasing an institution's ROI in IT. Indeed, it is a requirement for any institution-wide effort to reengineer instruction, student support services, and other administrative services. No institution can afford for long to operate parallel systems—the old way of doing business and the new, transformed way.

This principle of universal access has important ramifications for institutions of higher education, since students typically must bear the costs of their access to a personal PC—just as they now bear the costs of their personal access to an assigned textbook. They accordingly will expect the networked PC to be a necessary component of their learning environment and, thus, of the institution's instructional environment and student services environment. How to organize a lease or purchase plan for students is a topic in its own right (Graves, 1997b).

6. *An institution should contain overall IT support costs by centrally supporting only a few specific configurations of microcomputer hardware and productivity software, to be replaced or updated on a technological life cycle basis. Indeed, the central IT support organization should assume responsibility for the institution's IT architecture (standards) and organize departmental technical leadership to assist in the development of that architecture.* The universal access principle (Principle 5) implies continued growth in the use of IT, which in turn implies spiraling support costs in the absence of standardization. Universal access to Internet resources also implies that institutional standards should be consistent with the evolving standards and protocols of the Internet, such as those envisioned by the Internet2 Project and the federal Next Generation Internet Initiative. Standardization does not preclude the purchase and support of other technologies by departments, provided that such technologies do not increase the costs of central support for the shared network and its centrally supported baseline of applications. For example, every institution should have a uniform wiring plan and a set of guidelines for adding computers to its institutional network. These guidelines should assert the authority of the central IT support organization to deny or turn off network connections that imperil the reliability or robustness of the institutional network.

Winning agreement on a set of software tools for supporting the communications and resource needs of instruction is much more difficult than choosing a standard suite of office productivity software. Introducing a life cycle economic model will help make the case that standardization is desirable and will provide a basis for adding a seventh principle to the six discussed previously (the seventh principle is discussed later, in the section on the role of central IT services).

The Life Cycle Model

Investing wisely in IT is a tall order, especially when the pace of technological change is accelerating and technological expertise is scarce and difficult to hire, manage, and retain—or replace. An IT service provides a good institutional ROI when it can be affordably infused into the fabric of the institution to increase institutional effectiveness. Affordability does not necessarily imply cost savings, although it might. But affordability, in combination with infusion, does say something about the nature of the technology or service in question and its support. The technology or service must scale to broad-based institutional use, and in scaling beyond prototype use it must be supportable in an affordable manner. These are the characteristics of a commodity or core IT service, such as an institutional e-mail service or a set of Web-based services giving students access to institutional information about the academic and social services available to them, authenticated access to their transcripts, and authenticated access to instructional resources for their courses.

To take these ideas further, it will be useful to introduce a conceptual model for organizing and delivering IT services. This model is based on the concept of the life cycles of innovative products and services and is depicted and explained by Figure 5.1.[1]

Figure 5.1. Life Cycle Model.

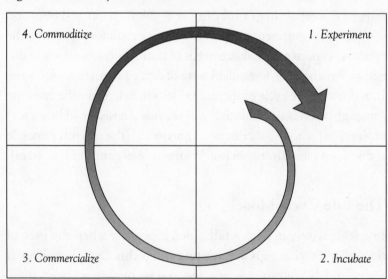

4. Commoditize   1. Experiment

3. Commercialize   2. Incubate

Most innovations that depend on technology evolve through four stages: experimentation, incubation, commercialization (or, in the nonprofit sector, implementation), and "commoditization"—the delivery of the product or service to the largest possible market at the lowest possible cost. In this model, experimentation and incubation costs are often high, so they must be shared or in some way subsidized. In contrast, commercialization (or implementation) and commoditization must be self-sustaining (or profitable, in the for-profit context)—often with some portion of the profits defraying the costs of the next life cycle of experimentation and incubation.

The Internet can be used as an example to elaborate these ideas. The Internet derived from a defense-related experiment and is evolving today into its next life cycle through the Internet2 Project, which is managed by the University Corporation for Advanced Internet Development and is a keystone in the federal Next Generation Internet Initiative. Figure 5.2 illustrates the Internet's evolution, described in detail in the following paragraphs.

Figure 5.2. Life Cycle Evolution of the Internet:
ARPAnet → NSFnet → Internet → BNS → Internet 2.

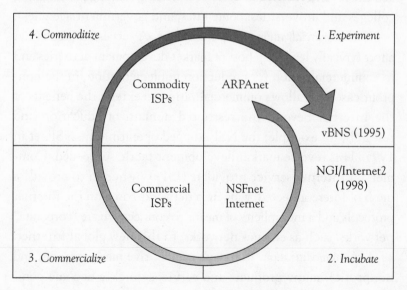

1. *Experimentation*. An innovative product or service often begins life as an experiment or a research study underwritten by a company or by some combination of commercial and nonprofit interests willing to share the precompetitive costs of creating new products and markets. The Internet, for example, can trace its origins to ARPAnet, an experimental network subsidized by the federal government, designed to connect a few computers serving defense-related research projects.

2. *Incubation*. An experiment or research study that points the way to a new product or service is often followed by an incubation period in which a viable prototype is designed and tested. In the case of the Internet, the National Science Foundation (NSF) recognized the potential of ARPAnet technologies to enhance research broadly in science and engineering, and accordingly it funded the NSFnet to support research and education among participating institutions. But NSFnet was also designed to demonstrate the scalability and affordability of inter-networks based on open standards and protocols. As the national backbone of the network of networks, which came to be called the Internet, the NSFnet exemplified the leverage to be gained by cost sharing (among participating colleges and universities, companies, and government agencies).

3. *Commercialization or implementation*. A successful incubation effort typically leads to a host of market development activities and to commercialization (or production implementation, in the nonprofit case). To allow commercialization to extend the benefits of the Internet beyond the restricted domain of education and research, for example, the NSF stopped operating the NSFnet in 1995. This reverse market development tactic succeeded. Commercial Internet service providers (ISPs) rushed in to provide a mesh of interconnected, wide-area networks based on the Internet protocols and a multiplicity of means to connect private "corporate" networks, such as campus networks, to this new global Internet.

4. *Commoditization*. In today's competitive markets (profit and nonprofit), many products and services quickly become com-

modities available not just to the corporate market but also to the consumer market—VCRs, PCs, institutional home pages, and the Internet itself are all examples. Recognizing that the potential value of the Internet is increased by every new connection, the commercial sector extended the benefits of the Internet to the ends of the public telephone network through the dial-up modem pool. Internet service is today a $10- to $20-per-month commodity, available from a new breed of ISPs operating in the consumer market wherever there is universal telephone service with reliable telephone connections. The next section, on prescribing the role of central IT services in the nonprofit academic community, describes core services that have the characteristics of commodity services—as affordable and accessible as possible to the broadest possible audience.

5. *The next life cycle*. Commodities usually breed low-cost competition, which leads to a search for value-added services and eventually to a competitive race into the next life cycle of innovation. The next life cycle of the Internet is well under way. In 1995, the NSF initiated the next life cycle of experimentation by connecting a few supercomputer centers through its very-high-speed Backbone Network Service (vBNS). Then, in 1996, the research university community announced the Internet2 Project (see http://www.internet2.edu/), an incubation-stage project, to capitalize on the vBNS experiment and other emerging advanced network technologies and applications. Shortly thereafter, President Clinton announced the federal Next Generation Internet (NGI) Initiative. NGI/Internet2 will demonstrate the scalability and economic viability of incorporating advanced technologies, such as the vBNS, into the Internet on a national level. Or, to use a software metaphor, NGI/Internet2 will be a mature beta version of the next release of the commercial Internet and, eventually, the commodity Internet.

The four successive quadrants of experimentation, incubation, commercialization-implementation, and commoditization provide a framework for increasing ROI in IT.

Prescribing the Role of Central IT Services

This section provides a new guideline, Principle 7, for addressing one of the three fundamental questions posed at the beginning of this chapter: "What should be the nature and scope of the services provided by a central IT organization, and how should that organization be organized to optimize its effectiveness?"

Principle 7 is as follows: *The heft of central IT expenditures should be directed toward implementing and providing baseline, core services through the implementation and commodity quadrants of the IT services life cycle.* Broadly available core services give the greatest bang for the buck. These services are also more mature offerings that benefit from the greater levels of management and control that can be offered by a central organization. At the other extreme, most central IT service organizations should dedicate only a small fraction of their resources to experimentation and incubation, for these activities carry considerable risk and often have high costs. A central IT organization should often find itself engaged with a department in incubating and implementing a new and promising technology. Instructional technology services, for example, might best be incubated in cooperation with one or two academic departments. Indeed, when possible, the central IT organization should let others assume or share the risks of experimentation and incubation and should take advantage of the leverage of investments made by others—vendors, academic and administrative departments, multi-institution collaborations, and so on. Figure 5.3 captures these ideas as a prelude to further explication.

What are the typical kinds of activities that would engage the central IT organization in quadrants two, three, and four of the IT support life cycle?

Quadrants 2 and 3: Selecting and Implementing Institution-Wide Core Services

The central IT organization should be deeply involved in institutional processes for selecting and implementing new IT services that

Figure 5.3. The Role of the Central IT Service Organization in the Life Cycles of IT Support.

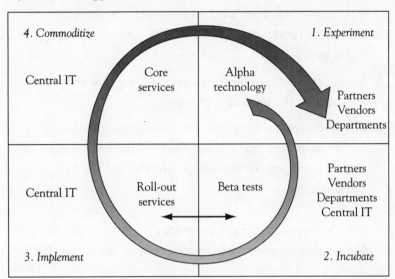

have the potential to become core services. Today's expectation should be that the central IT organization will

1. Establish lines of communication with departments to monitor both their emerging IT needs and the innovations that often arise from the entrepreneurial activities of their researchers or staff members

2. Organize and work with the technical leadership in departments to develop and maintain an IT architecture for the institution

3. Maintain relationships with vendors, to assess their newest products and upgrades

4. Participate directly in, or indirectly track, multi-institution collaborations and the programs of various research centers that are developing new standards or technologies with the potential to become mission-critical for the institution[2]

5. Participate, with veto power, in formal institutional processes by which new mission-critical systems (systems that support, for example, administrative and business operations and educational and outreach programs) are reviewed, vetted, and selected

6. Implement test beds for the most promising new services identified in the preceding processes

7. Plan and execute the initial implementation and the evolution to core production services of the new services that emerge from the preceding selection and test bed activities.

Some of these activities place senior IT officers in territory outside their authority, where only leadership can succeed—even when others involved expect authoritative solutions (Heifetz, 1994; Graves, 1997c). For example, IT officers do not have authority over instructional programs, yet they are often expected to provide central IT support for instruction that will meet the diverse instructional needs of highly differentiated academic departments. This dilemma demands a change management process in which the senior IT officer can play a role along with the "owners" of instruction. (This idea is further articulated in the later section on organizing and governing central IT services.)

Quadrant 4: Providing Institution-Wide Core IT Services

Core or baseline services are those that are available to every unit and most individual employees. Among the adjectives that should apply to these core services are *affordable, scalable, easy to use,* and *easy to support*—the attributes of commodity IT services with high-quality production values. These core production services define an institution-wide, economy-of-scale IT environment for communicating and for sharing information resources based on Internet protocols and other standards that enable global electronic communication and publication. In light of the previously elaborated principles, this means that today's expectation should be that the central IT service organization will

1. Install, operate, and upgrade the institutional network and its connection to the Internet

2. Install, operate, and upgrade other institutional communications networks for voice and video

3. Develop and upgrade institutional policies that describe the ground rules for connecting to and using the institution's data, voice, and video networks

4. Provide institution-wide support for acquiring a limited number of PC hardware-software configurations (through licensing and purchasing or leasing agreements)

5. Support the connection of these standardized PC configurations to the institutional network

6. Offer or arrange institution-wide training and continuing support for the bundled PC-software standards that provide access to a word processor, a spreadsheet program, e-mail, listservs, newsgroups, the World Wide Web, Web-based instructional tools and services, and mission-critical information resources and transaction processes (financial information and transactions, personnel information and services, information about the students, information and services for students, and so on) on an as-authorized basis

7. License and manage a set of server systems to provide the network-based services described previously

8. Participate in the migration from old to new core services

These activities are IT-owned operational processes, in contrast to the IT-related sociopolitical processes involved in selecting and implementing new IT services. This distinction between operational authority and process leadership can be reflected in a generalized model for organizing and governing central IT services.

Organizing and Governing Central IT Services

Many colleges and universities have created a senior IT position. In its most authoritative implementation, as stated earlier, this position is generally referred to as the chief information officer (CIO), in descriptive terms if not in the actual position title. The CIO is typically charged with overseeing the management of the central IT organization and providing leadership and coordination for the processes involved in identifying and introducing new IT services to reflect new technologies and new needs. Because the latter processes typically cross the boundaries dividing the responsibilities of the various senior administrative officers, it is strongly arguable that the CIO should report to the CEO. That is not always feasible, and in any case, the practical prerequisite for success is based on Principle 3: the CIO should fully participate in institutional planning and decision making at the cabinet level. Without a position with these responsibilities and a process to address a host of complex, institution-wide IT issues in parallel, an institution will not be able to create a holistic IT environment designed to ensure both effectiveness and efficiency from an institutional perspective and maximum flexibility from the point of view of the individual departments.

This analysis has addressed both the established core production IT services that are available institution-wide at any moment and the institutional opportunities and issues that must be addressed through collaborative processes designed to lead to coordinated direction and the development of new or replacement core services. Indeed, institutions need a governance structure that provides for the management of both core production services and the collaborative processes by which new services are selected and integrated into the production core—change management. For example, the selection of new administrative applications and the migration to these applications are processes that should have the participation of a diverse group of stakeholders if client support for such applications is eventually to be incorporated into the set of institution-wide core IT services. Similarly, the selection of centrally supported software tools to assist faculty efforts to use online communications tools and learning resources in instruction requires the broad participation of the academic departments and the support of academic leaders. The generalized schematic in Figure 5.4 provides an interpretation of the overall concept.

Figure 5.4. IT Core Services Management and IT Change Management.

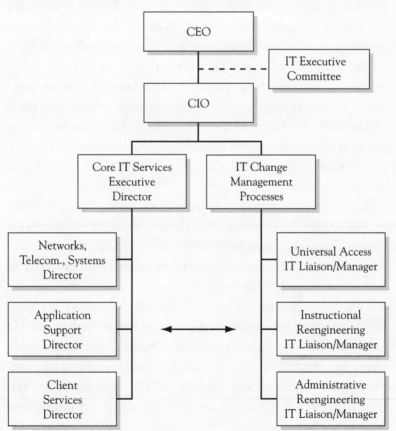

The two-way arrow symbolizes the need for an institutional process for selecting and implementing new or replacement core IT services (the arrowhead pointing to the left) and the need for the core IT services organization to participate in that process (the arrowhead pointing to the right)—and perhaps even to organize and staff such a process (the IT liaison-manager positions). The CIO is responsible for managing these relationships and for providing leadership for the inevitable institutional changes wrought by advances in information technology. The executive director is responsible for managing established core IT services that must be provided at all times on a reliable and scalable institution-wide production basis.

Under certain circumstances of institutional size and priorities, the responsibilities of the executive director and the CIO—operations management and change management—might have to reside in one person, but Figure 5.4 depicts a model preferred by many. Similarly, the demarcation of service areas on the left-hand side is but one example of how the fourth-quadrant activities listed earlier might be organized and managed—to focus on data, voice, video, and server infrastructure systems; mission-critical applications systems support; and client services such as help-desk and training services.

On the right-hand side, the three examples of change management issues are only illustrative (in today's terms) of the issues that most colleges and universities will continue to face in the immediate future. The importance of such issues argues for an executive or advisory committee to oversee the change management processes and outcomes facilitated by the CIO and the central IT organization—but not to the exclusion of other committee work directed at technical coordination and service improvement. Indeed, the three issues that introduced this chapter are bound together for institutions seeking to increase their ROI in IT by focusing it on their largest investment: the investment in instructional personnel and support for instruction.

The Special Case of Instructional Technology

The IT revolution, at its core, is a revolution in human communications enabled by the Internet. Seen in this light, it is easy to understand why academic research communities have led the way. Scholars and researchers organize themselves into highly specialized learned communities. These learned communities are rather homogeneous in terms of intellectual interests and academic preparation, and the Internet provides an opportunity to advance their highly refined common interests independent of place and time. Since the members of a particular learned community are typically dispersed across the globe, it is advantageous and natural for them to seize new opportunities for professional growth that supplement and enrich the traditional vehicles of conferences, sabbaticals, and journal articles.

In contrast, an instructor walking into a classroom on the first day of class is trying to create a new learning community from a group of students whose interest in the course (and one another) may not be wholehearted and whose abilities or academic preparation may be quite varied. It is more difficult to create a new learning community from such a diaspora than it is to participate in a well-defined learned community with like-minded and similarly skilled professionals. A good instructor-mentor is needed to motivate and facilitate a commonality of interest and purpose among disparate learners. Although seldom articulated as such, this is a key reason why many instructors who have embraced Internet tools to enhance their productivity as scholars still resist the use of the Internet as an instructional medium, because it risks dehumanizing the learning process. This resistance contrasts sharply to any faculty concern about the role of IT in research and scholarship, which is usually focused on acquiring more or leading-edge IT resources, not on any misgivings about IT as a professional tool for scholarly discovery and communication.

This line of thought that contrasts homogeneous learning communities with heterogeneous learning communities also suggests why instructors do not entirely resist—indeed, why they increasingly embrace—the use of online learning resources and communication tools in a traditional on-campus course in which classroom contact is ensured, providing a continuing opportunity to build common purpose through force of personality, or a career-oriented distance education course in which adult students' career goals and personal motivation, maturity, and circumstances help create a no-nonsense commonality of purpose and dedication to task.

The second of these scenarios is attracting a frenzy of attention because it offers possibilities for achieving economies in the cost, price, and convenience of education. In contrast, unless it is coupled with efforts to reengineer instruction, the use of online resources and tools in the traditional classroom context tends to add costs to education. In addition to these two economically different scenarios for using online resources and tools, however, are other possibilities that continue to engender considerable faculty resistance. These other possibilities include

- Reducing residency requirements for the traditional four-year baccalaureate experience

- Unbundling general education (liberal education) and mastery in a discipline or profession

- Decoupling the delivery of basic skills training (but not the necessity for it) from the baccalaureate experience

- Unbundling the delivery of content and the certification of competency, à la the Western Governors University model (Blumenstyk, 1998)

This resistance may owe to faculty recognition that new socioeconomic forces are beginning to reshape higher education into patterns that no longer appear holistic from the institutional perspective of today's colleges and universities but that are quite holistic from the perspective of national social and economic needs, including the student's. New online learning resources, online communication tools, and the ability to deliver student services online are at the heart of the new social expectation. Indeed, Internet communication tools are fast becoming sophisticated enough to address the social complexities inherent in this transformation. Enabled, for example, by Web discussion groups, these new communication environments, even more than the Internet delivery of content, account for—or should account for—the current interest in the deregulation and reshaping of higher education into educational micromarkets (Graves, 1997a; Heterick and Twigg, 1997). Although these educational micromarkets are based on a variety of nonprofit and for-profit financial models, the new tools for collaboration and group work are powerful across the spectrum of possibilities. They are as useful in the traditional on-campus instructional model as they are necessary in the distance education model. And the framework for increasing ROI in IT outlined here applies to the spectrum of instructional methodologies and economically differentiated educational delivery models, from the traditional classroom model to the new models enabled by the Internet's anytime, anyplace technologies.

From the ROI-based discussion of IT principles and life cycles, one point deserves emphasis across the spectrum of instructional technology planning. Principle 7 asserts, in the context of instruction, that a central organization typically should focus its IT expenditures not on developing instructional tools and new instructional models from scratch but rather on implementing and eventually providing core support services for instruction that have been developed and initially tested with the leverage of other interested investors—nonprofit or for-profit.

Instead, many institutions are today developing their own versions of an instructional technology environment that may easily lead to confusion and disarray, as thousands of HTML files accumulate with little regard for institutional coherence, scalability, and long-term manageability. This situation parallels, in many respects, an earlier era when institutions developed their own applications for administrative transactions and record keeping or toiled to customize off-the-shelf software to achieve the same impact. That era in IT-based administrative services is long gone. Many institutions now turn to contractors, not only to develop sophisticated and integrated modular administrative systems for the education marketplace and beyond but also to help implement and manage such systems. Such an approach can be a fruitful one in support of instruction as well.[3]

The idea is not to outsource the faculty but to outsource faculty development services and related technical support for instructional technology and the new instructional methodologies it enables. Contracting for faculty development services and related instructional technology support, like its counterpart for institutional administrative systems, can provide the leverage of national research and development activities enabled by profits or overhead accruing from multiple client institutions. This same R&D leverage protects the institution from technical obsolescence and affords it a smooth ride through the life cycles of instructional technology and instructional innovation. The institution can focus on the delivery of core instructional technology services rather than on the expensive R&D work that undergirds such services.

There is no doubt that every instructor will want to invent her own wheel, but that wheel must ride on a standard-gauge track, along with many other instructors' wheels, if the institution is to increase its ROI in IT and, more specifically, instructional technology. One way to achieve this is to contract institutionally with a service company or organization that focuses on faculty and institutional development services in the context of the use of online learning resources, online communication environments, and online student services in support of learning communities. At the very least, institutions should heed a variation on Battin's paradox: Internet technologies make possible unprecedented instructional innovation and unprecedented access to education, while at the same time requiring an institutionally coordinated set of faculty development services and related IT infrastructure support to permit the effective and affordable institutional exercise of that potential.

Notes

1. This model, in various formations, proved useful to the Internet2 Steering Committee in its attempts to place Internet2 in the context of the original Internet.

2. This envisions selective participation in national associations such as EDUCAUSE (http://www.educause.edu/) and the initiatives they spawn, such as the Coalition for Networked Information (http://www.cni.org/), the National Learning Infrastructure Initiative (NLII), the NLII's Instructional Management Systems Project (http://www.imsproject.org/), the Networking and Telecommunications Task Force, and the Internet2 Project (http://www.internet2.edu/).

3. Disclosure: The author recently joined a company, COLLEGIS, precisely to organize and offer such services to higher education.

References

Battin, P. "New Ways of Thinking About Financing Information Technology." In B. L. Hawkins (ed.), *Organizing and Managing Information Resources on Campus.* Educom Strategies Series on Information Technology. McKinney, Tex.: Academic Computing Publications, 1989.

Blumenstyk, G. "Western Governors U. Takes Shape as a New Model for Higher Education." *Chronicle of Higher Education,* Feb. 6, 1998.

Graves, W. H. "Free Trade in Higher Education: The Meta University." *Journal of Asynchronous Learning Networks,* 1997a, *1*(1) [http://www.aln.org/alnweb/journal/jaln_issue1.htm].

Graves, W. H. "A Framework for Universal Intranet Access." *CAUSE/EFFECT,* 1997b, *20*(2), 48–52 [http://www.cause.org/information-resources/ir-library/html/cem9729.html].

Graves, W. H. "Adapting to the Emergence of Educational Micro Markets." *Educom Review,* 1997c, *32*(5) [http://www.educom.edu/web/pubs/review/reviewArticles/32526.html].

Heifetz, R. A. *Leadership Without Easy Answers*. Cambridge, Mass.: Belknap Press, 1994.

Heterick, R. C, Jr., and Twigg, C. A. "Interpolating the Future." *Educom Review*, 1997, *32*(1) [http://www.educom.edu/web/pubs/review/reviewArticles/32160.html].

McClure, P., Smith, J., and Sitko, T. *The Crisis in Information Technology Support: Has Our Current Model Reached Its Limit?* CAUSE Professional Paper, no. 16. Boulder, Colo.: CAUSE, 1997 [http://www.cause.org/information-resources/ir-library/abstracts/pub3016.html].

Twigg, C. "The One Percent Solution." *Educom Review*, 1995, *30*(6) [http://www.educom.edu/web/pubs/review/reviewArticles/30616.html].

6

Tying Things Together

Advice for the Practitioner

Richard N. Katz and Associates

ollections of essays pose challenges to the practitioner. Unless
essayists are both carefully selected and well edited, the reader
is likely to be confronted by a great body of advice, much of it con-
flicting. Fortunately, the contributors to this volume share many
views. We hope that our collective experience and opinions, syn-
thesized and incorporated into the following summary, will provide
higher education leaders with a cohesive collection of approaches
to adapt to their particular campuses. Be prepared, however, to
reevaluate continuously and to adapt new programs as new competitors emerge, new technical capabilities prove themselves, and
the needs of students change.

Engage the campus in a vision. Colleges and universities are complex organizations. They are also organizations that thrive on the
exchange of ideas. To develop effective competitive strategies and
information technology investments, broad elements of the campus
community will need to align their efforts. Such alignment depends
on the widespread communication of, and agreement with, fundamental directions.

Inspire the organization to build a culture of learning that will
create environments for a lifetime of learning, transcending the
constraints of time and space. Understand that outstanding personal
education is your mission; focus on making education more effective by using computers to do what they do best, and free faculty to

devote more time to students on an individual basis. Do not lose sight of the higher purposes of the university.

Develop the capacity for change. Institutions that can step up to transformational change will have a much better chance of surviving than those that cannot. One of the most critical challenges will be to remove the constraints that prevent a quick response to new competitive pressures. Resistance to change can be overcome by situating new plans for enriching or extending the campus instructional program within understood and accepted planning and cultural contexts.

Communicate and act in ways that encourage the campus to embrace change as its greatest source of renewal. Assess the institution's real commitment to and sponsorship of change, as well as the readiness for change within academic units. Ensure that the campus policy infrastructures are capable of supporting the envisioned change. In particular, address early the very sensitive issue of who owns, manages, or coordinates the rights to course materials. Develop a shared view, and associated policies, of how new learning environments, processes, and products affect institutional rewards, image, access, quality, and cost.

Devise strategies. Few institutions will prosper under conditions of heightened competition solely on the basis of reputation. The realization of new opportunities will depend on the institution's ability to be agile. Agility will depend in turn on an articulated set of flexible strategies regarding curricular emphasis, target audiences, technical approaches, and the role of research and scholarship in the institution.

Focus your investments in instructional technology on the ten to twenty introductory courses that typically account for 40 to 50 percent of enrollments. Put in place three critical planning components: strategic guidelines and program development parameters, a rigorous business planning process for evaluating potential new ventures, and a rapid evaluation and decision-making process.

Develop the faculty. Faculty will need to be encouraged to reconceive their roles to become designers of learning experiences, processes, and environments. Such a reconception of roles must be accompanied by a rethinking of the incentive system for faculty participation in courseware development and production.

Consider bringing faculty rewards for pedagogy into greater balance with rewards for scholarship. Invest in pedagogical innovation: encourage faculty to go beyond the usual tweaking of established curricula and rethink how students are taught. Develop the institution's skills in managing effective partnerships—within the institution as well as externally with other institutions and private firms—to support new curriculum strategies. Provide faculty with substantial help in terms of staff support and equipment, allowing them to take advantage of the new media to improve education.

Manage IT as a strategic campus asset. Information technology is a strategic asset that can be utilized by the entire faculty, staff, and student body to increase the quality and productivity of campus academic programs and the administrative services that support these programs. The campus information technology vision and plans must be aligned with the evolving campus vision of instructional delivery, and the central IT organization must assume responsibility for communicating and reporting progress toward the institution's strategic vision for the deployment and use of IT.

Include in the development of your institution's strategies an assessment of the underlying technology requirements, a forecast of when needed technologies will be commercially mature and affordable, and an evaluation of technology risk. Involve the senior campus IT officer in institution-wide strategy setting and budgeting at the cabinet level. Ensure that central IT support is prioritized and funded to serve strategic institutional goals. Avoid reliance on one-time funding sources to pay for campus information technology.

Strive to make universal, convenient, and affordable access to personal computers, the Internet, and a basic collection of productivity software a reality for all students and employees. Watch for technological advances that your institution can exploit to make distant discussion and collaboration easier to use and more effective.

Support relatively few specific configurations of personal computer hardware and productivity software that will be replaced or updated on a technology life-cycle basis.

Enhance the institution's return on investment in information technology by directing the bulk of central IT expenditures toward implementing and providing broadly available core services. Whether these services are centrally or locally funded and managed, make sure that access to IT support is as accommodating and as near as possible to the individual. Strike a careful balance between central, institutional decision making and local, stakeholder-driven decision making in IT implementations. Develop implementation processes that involve central IT leadership, academic departments, and key faculty leaders in shaping an institutional approach to supporting the use of IT for both instruction and administration.

Focus on the assessment of student outcomes. Finally, as you begin to extend and enhance your institution's educational offerings, remember that the focus should continually be on the assessment of learning outcomes and on the quality and tenor of teaching and learning experiences.

Index